THE REGULATED EMIGRATION OF THE GERMAN PROLETARIAT WITH SPECIAL REFERENCE TO TEXAS

Being Also a Guide for German Emigrants

by Dr. Ferdinand von Herff

Member of the Darmstädter Colony on the Llano and at New Braunfels
1850

Translated
by
Arthur L. Finck, Jr.

Trinity University Press

San Antonio, Texas

The Trinity University Press gratefully acknowledges the assistance of Mrs. Ferdinand P. Herff in making this book possible in memory of the late Dr. Ferdinand P. Herff.

Originally published in German by Franz Varrentrapp Publishing Company, Frankfurt a/M, 1850.

Copyright © 1978 by Arthur L. Finck, Jr.
All rights reserved
Library of Congress Catalog Card Number 78-53527
SBN # 911536-72-8
Printed in the United States of America
Printed by Best Printing Company

To
June and Mark

FOREWORD

National ferment aroused by two world wars has limited widespread knowledge of the causes of nineteenth-century German emigration to the United States and the contributions of these people to the settlement of the country. Even so, scholars, especially in Texas and Wisconsin, have found this subject a fertile field for research. According to one count, more than twenty books relating to nineteenth-century Germans in Texas have been published since 1900. These studies tend to focus on a limited geographic area or a specific individual, however, and are based primarily upon material from the same kinds of sources: extant letters, memoirs of early settlers, local German-language newspapers, and records found in courthouses and the United States Census.

That so few American historians possess the linguistic talents to translate nineteenth-century German, the appearance of these contemporary sources in English usually portends a worthwhile contribution to scholarship. Further publication of translations, such as the one contained in this book, may be necessary before a definitive study by an American on the causes and immediate results of German emigration to Texas becomes available. The best general book remains Rudolph L. Biesele's *History of the German Settlements in Texas, 1831–1861* (1930). More specialized in its attention to agriculture and in a sense supplementing Biesele's work, would be geographer Terry G. Jordan's *German Seed in Texas Soil* (1966).

Although Biesele and Jordan expanded our knowledge of the motives for emigration, it was their bibliographies that alerted scholars to the extensive nineteenth-century German literature pertaining to colonization in the United States. Some fifty German publications had appeared in the 1830–1860 period, and approximately forty more volumes in the generation following the Civil War. Among the pre-Civil War publications, the principal works encouraging emigration that have been translated are those of Ferdinand von Roemer, Prince Carl of Solms-Braunfels, Gustav Dresel, Friedrich Wilhelm von Wrede, and W. Steinert, as has that of the well-known but unreliable Viktor Bracht.

No one of these advocates of German emigration developed such a systematic plan for the establishment of colonies, nor so enthusiastically favored Texas over Wisconsin as a location for settlement, as did Dr. Ferdinand L. von Herff in his *Die geregelte Auswanderung des deutschen Proletariats mit besonderer Beziehung auf Texas* (1850). No extant copy can be found in an American depository of this work by the man who would become a renowned surgeon in Texas. Professor Elisabeth Gütermuth of Nassau, Germany, through Mrs. Ferdinand P. Herff, happily brought to the attention of Trinity University Press a copy which she discovered in the *Landeshauptarchiv* of Koblenz.

Dr. Ferdinand L. von Herff, of a distinguished family, joined thirty-two other well-educated young men in the ill-fated Bettina experiment at the juncture of the Llano River and Elm Creek, Texas, in 1848. Bettina certainly did not possess the qualities of a "communistic" colony as we understand the term today, even though a number of sources have so described it. "Communal" would be a more appropriate adjective. As settler Louis Reinhardt recalled, Bettina "had no real government. Since everybody was to work if he pleased and when he pleased, the result was that less and less work was done."

Back in Germany following this Bettina experience, and with the full intention of returning to Texas forthwith, Herff prepared this manuscript in support of a large-scale government-regulated emigration of German proletariat to Texas. Unashamedly, Dr. Herff had only praise for the land to which he would return.

Herff's grandiose scheme of national support for emigration never reached fruition. As utopian as his dreams may appear, however, his basic concern, a means of livelihood for jobless Germans, was surely in the American pragmatic tradition. The vast lands of Herff's adopted state would offer new opportunities for the proletariat of many nations, and more than twenty thousand Germans, with or without government support, would find their way to Texas before the Civil War.

Donald E. Everett
Trinity University
San Antonio, Texas

ACKNOWLEDGMENTS

The story of the colony of Bettina on the Llano River has always been of special interest to me. Thus, when in a perusal of Dr. R. L. Biesele's study of the German settlements in Texas I came across a reference to a book by Ferdinand von Herff concerning the planned emigration of the German proletariat to Texas, I was immediately interested and embarked upon the project of translating this rare book.

I hope that the translation of this little volume will give those students of Texas history who are interested in the more obscure but often fascinating historical sidelights an opportunity to become acquainted with yet another such sidelight. The middle nineteenth century saw the zenith of the development of utopian schemes for finding a better and fuller life, and, while Dr. Herff protests his utter lack of faith in utopias, he could not entirely erase the idea from his book. The book is well written, but some of Dr. Herff's scholarly and complex sentences presented a challenge to the translator's knowledge of the German language. I hope I have been able to express in readable English the exact ideas of the author.

Those who assisted me in this project include Dr. R. L. Biesele, Mr. E. W. Winkler, and Ferdinand von Herff's grandson, the late Dr. Ferdinand P. Herff. I am grateful for their aid.

Arthur L. Finck, Jr.
Corpus Christi, Texas

CONTENTS

*Foreword by
Donald E. Everett · vii*

Acknowledgments · ix

*Introduction by
Arthur L. Finck, Jr. · xiii*

*The Regulated Emigration of the German
  Proletariat: With Special Reference to
  Texas by Dr. von Herff · 3*

Bibliography · 69

Ferdinand von Herff

INTRODUCTION
by Arthur L. Finck, Jr.

Ferdinand von Herff was born November 29, 1820, in the ancient city of Darmstadt, capital of the Duchy of Hesse-Darmstadt. According to von Herff's grandson Ferdinand Peter Herff, descendants of the Herff line trace their genealogy back to 1559. The family members converted to Protestantism about the middle of the sixteenth century, and, because of religious persecution, fled France to Belgium where they settled near Güttick. In Belgium the family continued to be harassed, this time by the persecutions of the Duke of Alva, and they were again forced to flee. They settled in Frankenthal and Frankfurt and changed their name from Herve to Heef or Heerff.

Ferdinand von Herff's grandfather was Vollrath Friedrich von Herff. The title evidenced by the "von" in the name was awarded the year before the grandfather's death. The father of Ferdinand was Christian Samuel von Herff, chief justice of the Supreme Court of Hesse-Darmstadt and writer on jurisprudence.[1]

After completing his course of study at the Gymnasium of Giessen, Ferdinand von Herff spent two years at the University of Bonn. Through his family connections he met many notable people, including Alexander von Humboldt, the renowned explorer and naturalist, and Prince Albert, Duke of Coburg, later

Introduction

Consort of Queen Victoria. Although von Herff's special interest lay in the field of natural sciences, especially botany, he decided to study medicine.

From Bonn, Herff went to the University of Berlin for two years to pursue his medical studies. He received his M.D. degree in March, 1843, from the University of Giessen, his home university, where by the law of the day he had to do his final work.[2] At the age of twenty-three he was appointed a surgeon in the Hessian Army, where his brilliant surgical work soon made him widely known. While in the Army he became the first man in the world to open a lung abscess successfully.[3]

During these years of the mid-nineteenth century, when Herff was a student and then in the military, Germany was experiencing social, economic, and political upheavals mainly brought about by advancements in industrial technology. The first great crisis came in the years after 1840 when the German middleclass, up to now self-reliant and independent, in large numbers became wage-earners.[4] Real wages declined, and a working day of twelve to fourteen hours did not provide for a decent existence. Among large segments of the population were reduced standards of living, fewer marriages and births, more deaths, more crime, and increased emigration. The feudal aristocracy, which was still the ruling class in Germany, did little to alleviate the situation.

Many students and graduates of German universities were deeply concerned with the rising tide of unrest and misery among the masses. They were equally distressed with the lackadaisical attitude of the German government toward reform. Disillusionment led to exodus and even before the situation deteriorated into outright conflict, thousands of Germans migrated to America.[5] Ferdinand Peter Herff wrote, "The impact of the great wave of emigration and the spread of socialistic propaganda rapidly involved all levels of German society. . . . Ferdinand von Herff did not long remain immune to the social epidemic. Though his sympathy did not prompt him to active demonstration, it soon led him to the ranks of the refugees."[6] Indeed, the prospect of emigration seemed more and more attractive to Herff and others, and thus it was that he, along with other university men, organized a movement to establish a settlement in America in 1847 which would become the colony of Bettina on the Llano River in Texas.[7]

Introduction

This settlement was made possible through aid received from the Society for the Protection of German Immigrants in Texas, a society of German noblemen who had received a grant of land in Texas. (The Society for the Protection of German Immigrants in Texas will be referred to subsequently as the "Society.") This Society, also known as the *Mainzer Verein*, or *Adelsverein*, first founded in 1842 but reorganized and chartered as a stock company in 1844, had as its object the promoting of German emigration to Texas.[8] It was instrumental in the founding of New Braunfels and Fredericksburg, but its activities were severely curtailed because of lack of capital and the ensuing indebtedness.

By 1846 several of the societies had been formed to aid in the colonization of Germans. There was in southern Germany another active society called the *National Verein für deutsche Auswanderung und Colonisation* (National Society for German Emigration and Colonization), whose purpose was to buy land in Wisconsin and to lead to it emigrants from Germany.[9] According to letters written by Count von Castell, director-general of the Society in Germany, the journals and newspapers of the time were actively working for this society in southern Germany and against the Society for the Protection of German Immigrants in Texas, printing all unfavorable letters that came out of Texas for the purpose of swaying public opinion against Texas as a suitable area of colonization.

Just previous to this agitation, there was organized in Darmstadt a company of young men, under the leadership of Hermann Spiess and Dr. Ferdinand Herff,[10] whose purpose was to found a colony in Wisconsin or Iowa,[11] a colony that was to be run on cooperative principles. Friendship, freedom, and equality would be the watchwords; no regular scheme of government was planned, since such a society would countenance no ruler.[12]

The Darmstädter company consisted of fewer than fifty persons, men of scientific and technical training as well as farmers and craftsmen. Spiess had traveled for some two years in the United States and returned convinced that Wisconsin and Iowa or the northwestern part of Texas offered the best area for settlement.[13] Apparently the members of the company had decided on Wisconsin before Count Castell, director-general of the Society in Germany, invited Spiess and Herff to visit him.

After consultation with Castell, Spiess and Herff decided to plan their colony in Texas on holdings of the Society.[14] Another possible influence might have been in the person of Prince Carl of Solms-Braunfels, the first commissioner-general of the Society in Texas and the founder of New Braunfels. Prince Carl spoke to the students of the Universities of Giessen and Heidelberg and to the students of the industrial school in Darmstadt of the greater opportunities for skilled and professional persons in a new and developing country and described Texas as the land of milk and honey, rich beyond imagination.[15]

Why this great interest in a small company of men from Darmstadt, many of whom held beliefs that must have been anathema to the princely officials of the Society? Count Castell himself said that he and the other members of the executive committee of the Society hoped that if the Herff colony proved a success, everything would be won for the Society. "They have the trust of their German countrymen, and if their settlement succeeds, there can be no doubt that the stream of emigration will be directed toward Texas and the price of our lands will increase in value," wrote Count Castell to John O. von Meusebach, the successor to Prince Solms as commissioner-general of the Society and a cousin of Herff.[16] Meusebach was ordered to do everything in his power to insure the success of the colony. If the colony, the first to be established on the actual grant of the Society, were to be successful, The National Society for German Emigration and Colonization would then step in and unite with the Society,[17] which would provide the Society with money enough to proceed with its plans. That is why Count Castell on February 11, 1847, at Wiesbaden signed an agreement with Hermann Spiess and Dr. von Herff, as representatives of the Darmstädter group, the terms of which are extraordinarily favorable to the independent company of adventurers from Germany.

According to the terms of the agreement, the Society pledged (1) to provide free transportation for the emigrants to the number of fifty and for their effects from Galveston to the grant, specifically, ten wagons with oxen; (2) to provide free provisioning of the emigrants until the first harvest; (3) to grant 320 acres of land to each emigrant; and (4) to provide emigrants with the necessary implements and materials for farming and handicrafts. To effect these guarantees, the gen-

Introduction

eral agent of the Society in Texas, Gustav Dresel, was authorized to draw upon the credit of the Society up to 30,000 guilders ($12,000). Spiess and Herff, as leaders of the group, were to get free transport to Texas and free board and lodging until the first harvest. Dr. Herff was pledged to furnish the group with medical attention. The colony was to be completely independent of other settlements already founded; also, Spiess and Herff were to be independent of any officials of the Society in Texas but had to report to the Director of the Society in Wiesbaden every three months. Since it was thought that at least 600 members were necessary for the success of the colony, the leaders could recruit members from other immigrants already in Texas, who were to have the same privileges under terms of this agreement. Furthermore, Spiess and Herff were allowed to choose the implements and materials necessary for the colony, and if these implements and transport were not available upon arrival at Galveston, they could make the purchase within the 30,000 guilders limit. To assure a place for the settlement in case the projected destination in the grant could not be reached, 500 acres were to be given the Bettina group at either Pedernales (Fredericksburg), Nassau Farm, or New Braunfels; these 500 acres were also guaranteed the members if the settlement were to fail. Spiess was to choose this tract with the stipulation that the 500 acres could not be in city lots. In case of the death of Spiess or Herff, Gustav Schleicher and Fritz Schenk were to take over their rights and duties.[18]

Very soon thereafter, Spiess, Herff, and Dresel left in advance of the company to make the necessary arrangements for the settlements. They departed from Liverpool on March 4, 1847,[19] landed in New York, and from there proceeded to Galveston. According to Reinhardt, the main group of thirty-two men sailed from Hamburg in April, 1847.[20] After seventy-eight days at sea, storms having delayed the beginning of the voyage,[21] the party arrived at Galveston. A letter written by one of the men in Galveston on July 13, 1847, and quoted in *Der deutsche Auswanderer*, a weekly journal of the time, stated that Galveston had almost six thousand inhabitants, much trade, and a large slave population. The writer mentioned the pretty farms, houses, and gardens, rank figs, cattle in the meadows, and hogs on the streets by the hundreds.[22]

Spiess had gone on ahead of the colonists, leaving Herff to

Introduction

guide them to their destination. The Society up to now had fulfilled all of its obligations to the Darmstädter group, but at Galveston wagons were apparently hard to get, so the party decided to go by sea to Indianola. The United States government pressed into service a schooner that was being readied to take the colonists to Indianola. The captain of this substituted ship ran the vessel on a sandbar; when he attempted to leave the disabled ship on the pretext of securing aid, Herff drew his pistol and forcibly detained him.[23] Among the colonists was a ship's carpenter named Kappelhoff who repaired the leak, and in five days the company reached Indianola.[24]

At Indianola two men, Vogelsang and the Canadian, Rock, joined the party. In the course of a few weeks the men reached New Braunfels where, two and one-half miles from the town, Spiess had chosen the 500-acre plot pledged them under the terms of the contract with the Society. Three stayed to care for the place, which became known as the "Darmstädter Farm,"[25] while the rest of the party continued on to the Llano,[26] guided by Emil Kriewicz, who was well-acquainted with the country.

On the north bank of the beautiful crystal-clear "Silvery Llano," as Reinhardt called it, just below present-day Castell,[27] they founded the settlement of Bettina. The colonists erected a temporary shed and later an adobe house covered with pecan wood shingles. By the end of November, 1847, a number of fields had been plowed and a ferry had been constructed over the Llano River.[28]

The relations of the colonists with the Indians during these months were very cordial, although at times there were 2,000 Comanches in the area. They looked on Dr. Herff as a medicine man, and one Comanche even offered him a young Mexican girl as a gift after the doctor had completed a successful eye operation on the Indian.[29] Dr. Herff described the Indians as unaggressive and noted that twenty men with good dogs could feel secure in Indian country.[30]

But these men of European learning had little practical knowledge of frontier life, and many began to avoid the hard labor. Although they managed to raise about 200 bushels of corn in 1848, the prospect of having to shift for themselves without aid from the Society after the first harvest caused some to leave the settlement, and, by fall, all the colonists had returned to the Darmstädter Farm.

Introduction

After the abandonment of Bettina, Dr. Herff left the group, traveled to Europe to marry his betrothed, Mathilde Klingelhöfer, intending to return to Texas immediately. At that time, however, Germany was in the throes of revolution and Herff, still an officer in the army, was impressed into service.[31] He married Miss Klingelhöfer, and, after his commission expired, they began their delayed trip to America, reaching their destination in April 1849. The Herffs located at New Braunfels, Texas, and the doctor immediately took out citizenship papers. One year later they moved to San Antonio where he enjoyed a long and remarkable career in the field of medicine.[32]

It was probably during the first few months after his return to Germany in 1848 that he wrote the manuscript of his book outlining his plan for the regulated emigration of the German proletariat to Texas. On August 7, 1849, he appeared before the Committee of the Society, upon invitation of Dr. Tabor of Darmstadt, to report upon conditions in Texas. The grant of the Society, he claimed, was naturally favored by nature and of especial value. Minerals such as zinc were to be found on the Llano. It had been demonstrated that crops could be grown there. His fellow colonists had withdrawn to New Braunfels but were anxious to return to the grant where cultivable lands had been left. Part of the blame for the failure to maintain the Bettina settlement lay with the Society, which had made only $3,000 of the promised $12,000 available to the settlers.[33]

Herff left his manuscript with the Committee members, who apparently decided to publish it in the hopes of inducing further emigration to Texas. Accordingly, they turned it over to Franz Varrentrapp, a publisher and bookseller of Frankfurt, and paid two hundred florins out of the Society treasury for the printing and distribution of the booklet.[34]

In this little book, Herff, after relatively lengthy introductory remarks, presented his scheme for a planned, orderly emigration of the German proletariat to Texas. It is surprising that the Herff manuscript was so well received by the Committee of the Society, since it was very critical of the way in which the Society administered its affairs in Texas. Possibly the Society felt that a straightforward exposition of conditions in Texas relative to German emigration by a well-known man not directly connected with the Society would be advantageous. Perhaps some members of the Society had suggested Herff write the book since he emphasized the need for a "national" society to take over the task of planning and directing emigration. In any event, Biesele pointed out in *German Settlements in Texas*, "It was not Dr. Herff's intention, however, to promote any system, idea, or principle of socialism, but simply to make the largest number of workers self-supporting in the least possible time and with the least possible expense."[35]

Herff wrote that emigration had become a national issue and that piddling, haphazard measures would no longer suffice. Something needed to be done so that, as economically as possible, the workers quickly could become independent and respectable citizens. The solution, Herff maintained, would be to plan and establish colonies upon extensive lands purchased for that purpose. Since this would require a great deal of money, only a national organization could put into effect such a program. Furthermore, he felt it would take the assistance of the various German state governments to accomplish anything worthwhile, and he suggested the use of the German fleet to transport the colonists.

Where should these colonists be settled? Herff had, of course, only America in mind and proceeded to make out a strong case in favor of Texas. No one could have been more partisan in his enumeration of the advantages of Texas than Herff: the climate of Texas was the most wholesome in the United States, land was cheap, and the basic necessities of life were available. These necessities could not only be bought at a very low price but could be obtained with a minimum amount of labor from a small quantity of land. In Texas the colonists would be able to get by with less labor and the time between their arrival and the first harvest was shorter than it would be in the northern part of the Union. On every count the advantage was with Texas as a place for settlement; besides, only in Texas had the practicality of large-scale colonization been proven.

Having built up an impressive argument for Texas as the site for the proposed colonization effort, Dr. Herff began the actual sketch for a proletariat colony in Texas. First of all, land must be acquired. The northwestern part of Texas, that is, the country between the Colorado and Rio Grande, he judged most suitable for colonization purposes. Land could be obtained through purchase from private individuals, through acquisition of headrights, or through acquisition of a government grant, the first

Introduction

being the safest, albeit the most expensive method. Care should be taken in choosing townsites, for the area offered great potentialities for manufacture and trade. Herff emphasized the possibility of engaging in trade with northern Mexico, which up to 1849 had been monopolized by traders coming in along the old Santa Fe Trail.

With such rich land in Texas a plot of ten acres would suffice for an average family of five. These ten acres should be an outright grant to the settler. The costs of the colonization enterprise could be repaid by reserving for the use of the colonizing society certain tracts of land and waterpower sites which would eventually be valuable as manufacturing sites.

In his plan for the actual colonization Herff presented a marvelously utopian scheme. He would send the colonists over by increments, to arrive in the colony at the right season of the year, providing them with provisions until the first harvest and with the necessary field and construction tools. The colony would be so regulated that the first increment of settlers would raise provisions sufficient for their own use and for the members of the succeeding increment. This would necessitate giving up part of what the first settlers raised to feed incoming settlers; therefore, this would require some sort of compulsion. Requiring as it did some surrender of absolute individual liberty, Herff argued that the security afforded the settlers as protégés of the colonizing society was enough to keep them in line, especially since being in a strange country they would be unlikely to wish to strike out alone.

Dr. Herff then went on to discuss in detail such matters as transporting the settlers from the seaport to the colony, provisioning them for the first year, supplying the necessary field and building equipment, and providing leadership of the settlers in the colony. Since his suggestion was to settle thousands of families at a cost that was not to be prohibitive, he considered the element of communal association in building houses, breaking the land, and using of tools and implements. To the principal criticisms of such a plan, Herff had an answer. He rejected the argument that it was impossible in practice to carry out such a plan and documented instances in which it had been done. Far from admitting in this book that the Bettina settlement had been a failure, he claimed on the contrary that such a plan in fact worked out very well at Bet-

Introduction

tina. To the criticism that the plan was detrimental to the liberties of the individual he rebutted that he was interested only in presenting what to him seemed to be the only practical way of dealing with the very pressing need at hand. In America, he maintained, one would have little chance of losing one's freedom through such a plan, and it might well be that the settlers after a year under such a cooperative system would voluntarily carry it on.

This little book published 128 years ago presented one person's opinion, albeit an opinion which carried some weight, as to how the serious problem of German overpopulation might be solved. Whether or not the publication of this book had any appreciable effect on the emigration of the 1850's would be difficult to determine. This grandiose scheme of national colonization envisaged by Herff never came to fruition, of course. Emigration continued at a high level during the decade following, but there was little that was "regulated" about it.

NOTES

1. Two sketches of the life of Ferdinand von Herff are available. One is in Ferdinand Peter Herff, *The Doctors Herff: A Three-Generation Memoir*, Laura L. Barber, ed., 2 vols. (San Antonio, 1973), pp. 3–130. The other is contained in Pat Ireland Nixon, *A Century of Medicine in San Antonio* (San Antonio, 1936), pp. 170–183. Information in the first two paragraphs of this essay is based on "The Family Von Herff" in *The Doctors Herff*, pp. xi–xiii.

2. M. J. Bliem, M.D., "Ferdinand Herff," *Southwest Texas Medicine* (March 1934), p. 10f. Years later, on the fiftieth anniversary of his graduation from Giessen, his alma mater honored him with a Jubilee degree.

3. Ferdinand P. Herff to Arthur L. Finck, Jr., May 9, 1949. In *The Doctors Herff*, Herff wrote, "His successful opening, draining, and subsequent care of tuberculous pulmonary abscess was only one of many such daring achievements. Never having been successfully accomplished before, this operation was reported in the Rhenish Archives, creating a sensation which greatly heightened the young surgeon's prestige . . . ," p. 6.

4. Valentin Veit, *The German People, Their History and Civilization from the Holy Roman Empire to the Third Reich* (New York, 1946), p. 403.

Introduction

5. Herff, *The Doctors Herff*, p. 8.
6. Herff, *The Doctors Herff*, pp. 8–9.
7. The settlement was named after the friend of Goethe, Bettina von Arnim.
8. Rudolph L. Biesele, *History of the German Settlements in Texas 1831–1861* (Austin, 1930), pp. 66–69. This society had acquired the Fisher-Miller Grant above the Llano River in Texas, but had made no settlement within the limits of the grant itself prior to 1847. The Bettina Colony was to be the first settlement in the grant; New Braunfels and Fredericksburg were settled earlier, but were not located on the grant.
9. Count Carl von Castell to L. Cappes, Wiesbaden, Germany, February 8, 1847, in *Solms-Braunfels Archiv*, XLIX, 187–188. See also *Solms-Braunfels Archiv*, LXVIII, 68ff. This Archive consists of seventy typescript volumes compiled under the supervision of Professor Rudolph L. Biesele and deposited in the Archives of The University of Texas.
10. Herff in *The Doctors Herff* said that Ferdinand joined a fellow graduate of Giessen, Gustav Schleicher, in organization of a society, *Die Vierziger*. But he also said that von Herff and Hermann Spiess embarked from Hamburg for New Orleans earlier than the other to facilitate arrangements and purchase supplies (pp. 9–10). The agreement with the Society is written in terms of Herff and Spiess as leaders (see pp. xvi–xvii).
11. *Solms-Braunfels Archiv*, XXVIII, 9.
12. Louis Reinhardt, "The Communistic Colony of Bettina," in *The Quarterly of the Texas State Historical Association*, III, 34.
13. *Solms-Braunfels Archiv*, LXVIII, 112.
14. *Ibid.*, XXVIII, 9. Herff makes no mention of this choice between Wisconsin and Texas in *The Doctors Herff*.
15. Reinhardt, "The Communistic Colony of Bettina," 33. This influence is also referred to in *The Doctors Herff*, p. 9 and in Biesele, *German Settlements in Texas*, p. 154.
16. Count Carl von Castell to John O. Meusebach, Wiesbaden, Germany, January 28, 1847, in *Solms-Braunfels Archiv*, LII, 245.
17. *Ibid.*, 252.
18. *Solms-Braunfels Archiv*, XXVIII, 11–16.
19. *Ibid.*, XLIX, 189.
20. Reinhardt, "The Communistic Colony of Bettina," 35.
21. *Solms-Braunfels Archiv*, LXIX, 117.

22. *Ibid.* Reinhardt's date of arrival, July 17, is obviously in error, since this letter was written in Galveston on July 13.
23. Herff quotes von Herff as telling the captain, "If this ship sinks, you Mr. Captain, will sink with it!," *The Doctors Herff*, p. 12.
24. *Ibid.*
25. Adolf Paul Weber, *Deutsche Pioniere* (San Antonio, 1894), pt. I, 27.
26. Biesele, *German Settlements in Texas*, p. 156.
27. Castell was founded shortly after the Bettina Colony by thirty families who also at first worked cooperatively. Bene, in a letter to the Executive Committee of the Society, located the settlement two miles above Bettina, which was situated at the point where the Elm Creek flows into the Llano River. Louis Bene to Count Carl von Castell, New Braunfels, Texas, November 23, 1847, in *Solms-Braunfels Archiv*, XLIX, 9.
28. *Solms-Braunfels Archiv*, XLIV, 9; LXIII, 121.
29. Weber, *Deutsche Pioniere*, 30–31. Also Herff, *The Doctors Herff*, p. 15.
30. *Solms-Braunfels Archiv*, XXXIX, 134.
31. Herff, *The Doctors Herff*, pp. 20–22.
32. Herff, *The Doctors Herff*, pp. 33–130 *passim*.
33. *Solms-Braunfels Archiv*, XXXIX, 133–137.
34. *Solms-Braunfels Archiv*, XXXIX, 144, 176.
35. Biesele, *German Settlements in Texas*, p. 6–7, n. 15.

*The
Regulated Emigration
of the
German Proletariat
With Special Reference to
Texas*

Facsimile of title page from *Die geregelte Auswanderung des deutschen Proletariats mit besonderer Beziehung auf Texas* (The Regulated Emigration of the German Proletariat with Special Reference to Texas), originally published by Franz Varrentrapp's Verlag, Frankfurt a. M., 1850.

Die

geregelte Auswanderung

des

deutschen Proletariats

mit besonderer Beziehung auf

Texas.

Zugleich ein Leitfaden für deutsche Auswanderer

von

Dr. von Herff,
Mitglied der Darmstädter Niederlassung am Llano und bei Neubraunfels.

Frankfurt a/M., 1850.
Franz Varrentrapp's Verlag.
Ph. Krebs.

The Regulated Emigration of the German Proletariat: With Special Reference to Texas

by Dr. von Herff

The question of emigration has in recent times acquired such significance that it has become a national issue. The German Parliament[1] in a bill introduced during its session, several German state governments through grants of money, and a few communities through support of poorer emigrants have tried partially to solve this problem and through such action have approached that remote objective. It was chiefly the parliamentary bill, about which one of the most prominent of those having the right to vote on the emigration question (the Hon. v. Gagern *sen*[2]) has acquainted me for this purpose, which in-

---

[1] Herff undoubtedly here has in mind the Frankfurt national assembly, a popularly elected body representing all German states and made up of both liberals and revolutionaries, which met on May 18, 1848, to draw up a constitution under which all German states might be united in a national confederation. Its purpose was not achieved. Thirteen months after it convened it broke up because of pressure from the counterrevolutionary forces, and its remaining members were finally dispersed by soldiers of the Württemberg government. Ernest F. Henderson, *A Short History of Germany*, II (New York, 1916), 353–369.

[2] Baron Heinrich von Gagern, Sr., foreign minister of the Electorate of Hesse, was president of the Frankfurt Parliament of 1848–49. Von Gagern was greatly interested in emigration to America and was a member of the executive Committee of the Society for

duced me to write down the following observations concerning a regulated national emigration. My two-year sojourn in the United States should justify my comments since I am projecting not just my own ideas, but am drawing from the sum of facts, experiences, and results which my close acquaintance with the particulars of the colonizing operation of such a grandiose scale in the Union (that of the Mainzer-Verein[3]) has placed at my disposal.

The bill of the German Parliament before me indeed covers all of those points which relate to emigrants who can take care of their own transportation and themselves defray the costs of emigration and to their protection against possible fraud at the hands of emigration agents as well; but it leaves out just that point which is of the greatest importance, namely, the concern for the actual proletarian.

Merely providing him [the emigrant] with free transportation cannot begin to help him; an organization for emigration to North America must be established here. Neither the obligations which the old fatherland has toward nor the demands which the new fatherland has on the emigrant can be complied with if the activity of the leaders of the emigration is limited to disembarking each year a certain number of people, helpless and destitute, upon the distant shore. It does not absolve the obligations of the old fatherland to lead thousands of its children into so hopeless an existence as that which stares the completely destitute German proletarians in New York and New Orleans in the face. It is not to the best interests of the new fatherland if a foreign nation ejects its surplus, or perhaps its refuse, population onto the hospitable shore without according them the means to establish an independent livelihood.

One who has closely observed the people (not all consisting of actual proletarians) who are daily disembarked in the coastal cities of the United States will not condemn the American government if it does not welcome the all-too-heavy throng of

---

the Protection of German Immigrants in Texas. Henderson, *A Short History of Germany*, II, 354; *Solms-Braunfels Archiv*, XXX, 38, LXVIII, 6off.

[3] The Society for the Protection of German Immigrants in Texas (*Verein zum Schutze deutscher Einwanderer in Texas*) was also known in Germany and among the German settlers in Texas as the Mainzer-Verein or Adelsverein. See Introduction, page xv.

destitute emigrants and passes general regulatory laws against them. The helplessness, the begging, in short the whole sum of the results of the physical and moral instability of the multitude, who were thrust out of their fatherland and are unwelcome in the foreign land, is most glaringly evident in the chief seaport cities of the North and South: New York and New Orleans. One can read daily the notices of corpses of unknown strangers over whom the coroner has pronounced the verdict, "Died of hunger and exposure." Almost as many reports of thefts, burglaries, breaches of peace, and drunkenness fill the columns of the police blotter. Already there has arisen, motivated to be sure by other ignoble motives, the so-called "Native party,"[4] demanding a stricter naturalization law, as well as either a bond of $250 from each immigrant or the assurance that he will be able to earn his own living without becoming a burden to the country. The two-year-old law which regulates the number of passengers per tons displacement of immigrant ships is proof already that the disadvantages of a European proletariat forced upon America is fully realized.[5] The almost unanimous indignation of all transatlantic newspapers on the occasion of the well-known Grosszimmer case proves that those who believe the refuse of Europe is welcome in America are in

---

[4] Various of these "Native" parties arose throughout the United States during the second quarter of the nineteenth century, culminating in the formation during the latter 1840's of the so-called "Know-Nothing" or Native American Party. The other "ignoble" motives of which Herff speaks were the antipathy toward Catholics and the anti-foreign feeling. An important element contributing to the rise of nativism was the fear of economic competition from the immigrants, and, as early as 1819, the Society for the Prevention of Pauperism in the city of New York called attention to large numbers of paupers among the immigrant population and to the expense of caring for them. The Native American Party demanded a stricter naturalization law extending the required period of residence to twenty-one years. Alice Felt Tyler, *Freedom's Ferment* (Minneapolis, 1944), 374–377.

[5] By an act of February 22, 1847, Congress limited the number of passengers to two per five tons displacement of passenger ships. This proviso was repealed by a subsequent act of May 17, 1848, which, however, provided for the proper ventilation of such ships and increased the amount of superficial deck space per passenger. These regulations were passed to maintain passenger health, and they did not seem to be an attempt to limit immigration as Herff infers. George Minot, ed., *United States Statutes at Large*, IX (Boston, 1857), 128, 222–223.

error. How much higher will these disapproving voices be raised, if, as a result of German national legislation, the transportation of completely destitute and, I am sorry to say, mostly undisciplined persons will increase, perhaps a hundred-fold.

The bill to be sure contains a passage which indicates that the necessity of transatlantic aid for the emigrant has been recognized. It proposes the appointment of German consuls, as well as contemplates the furnishing of aid such as that which has been tendered by the German societies which have existed for a number of years in New York, New Orleans, and other places.

Unfortunately this remedy is but a very insufficient one. Unless provided with the large amount of capital necessary for the planning of emigration beyond the sea, the consuls can only advise, and, at most, protect against violations of international law. On the other hand, the German societies are highly respectable, of course, and in their small sphere very beneficent institutions, but they too completely lack capital that is anywhere near adequate. Since their existence depends solely on voluntary contributions, their chief activity is the giving of advice, which up to now a disproportionately small number, in relation to the great number of immigrants, have taken advantage of, as inferred from annual reports.

It is therefore necessary to find some other expedient that will offer to the emigrants an operational basis that will enable them through their own labor to become self-dependent and respectable citizens in the new homeland in the shortest possible time at the lowest possible cost to the mother country. This one and only expedient is the planned establishment of colonies, effected by the purchase of extensive lands. The chief problems which must be taken into consideration in such an undertaking are:

1) Selection of a territory where, along with a healthy climate, the land is cheap and of great fruitfulness.

2) Choice of a territory which offers the new arrivals not merely a material existence, not merely the comfortless life of farmers and shepherds producing their own simple needs, but also the advantages which the resulting industry and trade and their attendants, spiritual uplift and knowledge, afford them because of location and even more because of the nature of its products.

3) Establishment of the colony according to a principle whereby, if not all, then at least the major portion of the costs incurred therein pay for themselves.

4) Practical, simple, and energetic leadership of the transplanted masses, whereby the acquisition of the basic necessities of life can be assured and a higher standard of living established, but with a limited administrative personnel, the least complicated daily business routine, and the greatest possible avoidance of anything that resembles impracticable guardianship of everyone in America.

Above all, money is necessary to the carrying out of every colonization project, and not in any small amounts as was the case with the late Mainzer Verein, but *a sum fully adequate for the original requirements and available at the right time.* Only with an immediately available large operating capital does one certainly and economically achieve his purpose as well as have a greater assurance of the restoration of the costs through the undertaking itself. Four horses hitched together to one wagon will pull it easily; if one, however, allows one horse after another to exhaust his strength pulling the wagon alone, horse and wagon will perish. This was the error, indeed the basic fault, of the Mainzer Verein. Led astray by false reports, the *Verein* began its undertaking with a most insufficient capital and thereby soon experienced the tragic results of the paralysis of the actions of the officials, loss of opportunity, loss of credit, and disorderly management. The emigrants were subjected to misery, the officers to slander, and the shareholders to loss of money; whereas, with the right management, great things could have been achieved with the sum of 1½ million[6] which was successively spent.

The false notion that one can accomplish something in America with European *kreuzers*[7] is too prevalent to pass over entirely with silence. I have before me a plan whereby 255,750 guilders will establish three thousand families on 16,000 acres

---

[6] Guilders or florins. The capital of the Verein was in terms of guilders, one guilder being worth about forty cents.

[7] A minor South German and Austrian coin, originally of silver but later of copper, the *kreuzer* was worth about half a cent. Comparable to the English farthing or American penny, it was perhaps the smallest unit of German money known to Herff; therefore, it was here used in a figurative sense. *Webster's New International Dictionary*, second edition.

of land in Iowa and even make possible the share payment of 814 guilders per family (apparently from the wealth which an emigrant can earn on four acres of land in Iowa!). Provisioning during the first cropless year, aid in the matter of implements and the like—in fact none of the main factors relating to a colony for the poor—are even discussed; the hopeless ignorance about American conditions, apparent in every line, is brought out by the fact that even hunting and fishing rights and leases are discussed.

But who can raise the necessary sum of money that is really needed? My firm opinion is that without the active assistance of the various German state governments and without considerable contributions from the community treasuries it will be utterly impossible to accomplish anything worthwhile in this field. Philanthropic societies to which we are so easily inclined, but to which we contribute but little, are completely insufficient. One cannot compare our conditions with the English or American where practically all institutions for the public good emanate from private societies, such as the Antislavery Society, the Bible Society, the missionary societies, and others; Germany has neither the capacity nor the means nor that sixth sense of the Anglo-American stock so necessary to any exercise of "self-government" and will, of course, not acquire them as quickly as the urgency of the conditions relating to the emigration issue demands.

The governments and the various communities must share in the control of any emigration actually benefiting the proletariat; whatever private persons and philanthropic societies contribute in the way of financial aid will be a welcome and useful assistance. But the real mission of the latter will be to furnish a moral impulse and to defend and popularize the measures of the governments which will surely soon be fought and made suspect by a malevolent opposition.

The labor and burden of a regulated emigration may possibly be divided between the governments (central) and the communities in such a way that the former would take over the transportation and the latter the direction of the transatlantic existence of the emigrants. The German fleet can do the fatherland no greater service than to do away with the most tragic of all wars, civil war, by removing without bloodshed its causes in taking over the transportation of the proletariat. Part of the costs of so doing have to be borne anyway because of the very existence of the fleet and in part can be somewhat moderated by the following methods:

1. By preparing steerage accommodations[8] and saloon accommodations for those passengers who are able to pay their fares. With a great inclination to emigrate prevalent among the middle classes who see their modest existence threatened and among many of the wealthier families who are being uprooted because of the political conditions,[9] this measure may yield a good profit, especially if the rates are set so that all competition will be helpless.

2. Through the return cargo of the products of the country: cotton, tobacco, wool, hides, and others, on which the freight charges must not be excessive, and by which the confidence of the merchants, at all events, could be increased through an insurance company with reasonable rates, to be organized by the government. Naturally, as soon as these vessels are converted into emigrant-transports the crews should be only as large as the care and maneuvering of the ships require; certainly not so large as the crew of a vessel at full strength for actual wartime services, otherwise there would be very little room left for the emigrants. The vessels which the English government uses as transports to New Sidney can serve as a pattern. The transatlantic existence of the emigrants, that is, the real work of colonizing, must be undertaken by the separate communities, either each one by itself, or, what would answer the purpose better, according to a joint plan including all Germany. Simplicity of management, lower costs, and faster execution of the colonizing enterprise would be ample compensation, in the final analysis, for the great difficulty of uniting thousands upon thousands of special interests into a single purpose. A joint treasury, into which the contributions from

---

[8] For the proletariat, presumably, who were not able to pay their fares and therefore would have to be content with the inferior steerage accommodations in the lower decks.

[9] The liberal, republican movement in Germany, which had brought about the revolutions of 1848, was at this time succumbing to the political realities of resurgent autocracy. By the middle of 1849, the hopes raised for a united liberal Germany by the Frankfurt Parliament were dashed. Many of the more radical liberal patriots were of the middle classes; it was these, presumably, that Herff had in mind.

each community, based on the number of persons which it annually wants to send, are paid, the centralization of administration in a board of directors chosen by the separate communities, and, finally, the great advantage of being able to begin operations and immediately with a large operating capital—all of these reasons would justify the calling of a general convention, to which a certain number of communities would send a deputy, and in which joint measures for the great task, which reminds one of the work of cleaning the Augean stables,[10] of getting the illiberal communities to participate in a national undertaking, could be discussed. Several examples during the last ten years have already shown that the sending of destitute members of the community at the expense of the community treasury has been looked upon by the remaining inhabitants mainly as a favorable speculation. There are in Germany very few communities completely without means, and in general the communities are well enough off so that the expenses of an undertaking such as is proposed can easily be raised. The community wealth is not getting any larger whereas the proletariat is, and that in disproportionate progression. The consciousness that by his work, whether manual or mental, one can arrive at the place where one need not work merely for his daily bread, but rather for the sake of work itself, for the good of society, for the respect which comes from honest toil—this consciousness spurs the spirit and exalts the heart. It is different with the man who sees scarcely any possibility of ever working himself out of the restraining orbit of a wage earner's life; he lacks the zeal to labor, the motive of ambition, which is more powerful than the pangs of hunger. The proletarian becomes lazy, he becomes base, he transmits these characteristics to his children, and thus the fuel is being piled up in the bosom of the community which will catch fire at the least impulse from without and destroy the security of the peaceful citizen. It would thus be—without considering other reasons, without considering the possibility of a partial restoration of the expended sums—of great

---

[10] In Grecian mythology, the sixth of the Twelve Labors of Hercules, performed at the command of Eurystheus. Hercules cleaned the stables of Augeas, which housed 3,000 oxen and had not been cleaned for thirty years, in one day by diverting the course of the river Alpheus through the stables. M. A. Dwight, *Grecian and Roman Mythology* (New York, 1855), 315–318.

advantage to the communities, especially for the wealthier communities, which generally contain the largest number of poor members, to be rid of the proletarians. But there is also in most cases a financial advantage connected therewith. The burden of caring for the poor, which affects not only the community wealth but which annually consumes a considerable sum in the form of alms, gifts by charitable organizations, and collections contributed to by individuals, would cease for the most part. But particularly the share of the corporate wealth which the emigrating proletarian gives up in most cases would compensate richly the remaining members for the expended sums. I know of a community in our province of Starkenburg which is distinguished by its vagabond and mendicant proletariat. Its community property consists mostly of forests of such value that, if it were divided among the members of the community, the beggar who now wanders about homeless would receive as his share some twelve hundred florins.[11] It would take only one-sixth of this sum, if efficient use were made of it, to fully suffice to establish an independent existence for him in a transatlantic colony. But not even this amount need be completely lost. If the colony were laid out so that from the sale of certain tracts of land and local natural resources, such as waterpower and others that would increase in value enormously in a short time because of the development of the neighboring regions, the original expenditures would largely be refunded, the profit to the community would be still greater, and the expended sums would in relation to the result achieved be extremely insignificant.

It will not do at all, however, to begin with insufficient capital, since it is the beginning of the undertaking which demands a sum disproportionately larger than the further pursuit of the undertaking. If that sum is lacking at the right time, nothing will be accomplished, and the same conditions which hurt the Adelsgesellschaft[12] and almost completely defeated their plan will also deal this undertaking the death blow. Therefore I must

[11] The Austrian florin, also called gulden or guilder, was a silver coin, worth 40.2 cents, according to the tariff of 1848. Viktor Bracht, *Texas im Jahre 1848* (Elberfeld und Iserlohn, 1849), 220.

[12] Literally, "Society of Nobles." It was another name for the Society for the Protection of German Immigrants in Texas. See page xv in the Introduction.

again urgently call attention to a concentration of money power through the combining of the communities in a national emigration congress and maintain that every separate action of individual communities is wasted effort. I now come to one of the most important points, that is, the destination of the emigration. It is, of course, understood that I have only the North American free states[13] in mind, since I am well acquainted with these and therefore have an opinion on the subject. Whether or not and in what manner the Danubian kingdoms would be suitable for the execution of a national emigration plan is a question which I will leave to those men who are more intimately acquainted with the resources and statistical situation of those lands; however, I believe that the last named countries are in no way suitable for the requirements of a colonization site and that therefore the wide expanse of the Union must be made use of. And, after careful consideration and personal first-hand inspection of the different land areas of the United States, I definitely decided for Texas, and I want to advocate this view, which has recently become rather unpopular,[14] on the following grounds:

1) *Wholesomeness of the climate.* No part of the Union, with the possible exception of the mountainous districts of western Pennsylvania, western Virginia, eastern Tennessee, and eastern Kentucky, can compare to the western, by far the biggest, portion of Texas. The purity of the air and the moderate average annual temperature put Texas in every respect ahead of Wisconsin and Iowa, the beloved favorites of the friends of the North. The climate of the American continent is characterized—and this makes it so irritable to Europeans—by the great extremes in seasonal temperature, as well as the quick change-over from warm to cold, and vice versa. New York, Ohio, Illinois, Iowa, and Wisconsin have an Italian heat in summer, since during that season of the year the sun (unhindered by any north wind from the icy seas) can put forth fully as much heat

[13] Herff, like most German immigrants, was not interested in settling in territory subject to slavery. Probably he considered the western part of Texas unfit for slavery and therefore nominally free territory, for he certainly must have known that Texas in 1849 was a slave state.

[14] As mentioned in my Introduction, the journals and newspapers of the time apparently were negative toward Texas as a suitable area of colonization.

as in the latitude of Rome and Naples. Days of 28-30° R. +[15] in the shade are therefore no rarity in those regions, and the dearth of air currents as well as the humidity arising from the dense forests and countless lakes and streams, make it even more intolerable and uncomfortable. Even though Texas lies farther south than these states, the heat of the sun does not increase, and +30° R. is likewise the highest temperature which I and several diligent observers have noted over a period of years. On the other hand, it is different in winter. In the northern states there blows at that season the icy north wind; not tempered by any ice-free sea, it roars across the bare steppes and snow-covered plains of Labrador and the Hudson's Bay lands and brings the cold of the perpetual ice of Melville Sound and the Ice Sea to the South. Days of 21-23° cold[16] often follow the warm summer and fall days after barely an eight-day interlude, and a six-months-long winter can change just as rapidly into summer. In Wisconsin two years ago, the ice on the Fox and Milwaukee Rivers did not break up until April, and Dr. Wunderly, a physician whom I met there,[17] in a letter dated the 14th of May mentions the fact that the first spring plants were just then coming up. It is quite different in Texas. Here the north wind has lost its great strength, and the thermometer rarely falls below zero,[18] this only for a few moments before sunrise, so that neither lasting ice nor snow can be built up, and the thin frost that at times appears at that hour of the day in winter must succumb to the first rays of the sun. Now I ask,

[15] Dr. Herff uses the Reaumur scale. This thermometric scale was invented by the Frenchman, Rene Antoine Ferchault de Reaumur, about 1730, and is still used to some extent in France, Germany, and Russia. It is so graduated that 0 degrees marks the freezing point and 80 degrees the boiling point of water. To convert the above reading to Fahrenheit, it is multiplied by 9/4 and 32 added, thus being equal to 95–99.5 degrees Fahrenheit. The + sign indicates degrees of heat above zero.

[16] This is a minus reading, or degrees of cold below the freezing point of water; therefore, using the conversion formula, it is equal to a reading of -15.25 to -19.75 degrees Fahrenheit.

[17] After landing in New York in the spring of 1847, Dr. Herff, traveling as advance agent with Hermann Spiess and Gustav Dresel for the Bettina company, must have journeyed to Galveston via Wisconsin in order to have met Dr. Wunderly (Wunderlich?) at that time.

[18] Here again, the Reaumur scale is used, zero being equal to 32 degrees Fahrenheit.

which more nearly corresponds to the European climate, the basic characteristic of which is not the prevalence of winter but rather the uniformity of the summer and winter temperature? Is it the North? Or is it not Texas?

The largest portion of the Union consists of virgin forests traversed by streams, lakes, and marshes with the separate settlements established in the clearings. Dampness and vaporizations from the humus-rich soil, which no beneficent sea breeze carries away during the summertime, cause dreaded autumn fogs with their attendants, bilious fever and the ague, which afflict the new settlers in Illinois, Wisconsin, and Iowa. West Texas, on the other hand, is hilly country, which rises terrace fashion from the coast, as rich in prairies as in woodland, without marshes, and regularly swept by sea breezes out of the south-southwest [sic]. The ague and bilious fever, in fact all those autumn sicknesses prevalent in the Mississippi, Ohio, and Missouri river basins, are practically unknown west of the Colorado. American doctors are well aware of this and send their patients suffering from liver and lung ailments and their dropsy and fever patients out of Illinois and Indiana to Texas. If one compares the pallid coloring, the bloated look, of the inhabitants of Illinois and Wisconsin, who live under the influence of the forest air, with the robust red of the Texans, there is no doubt where it is healthiest. Only eastern Kentucky and the previously named hilly regions of the Union are similar in that respect, and I have often heard an old Kentuckian, who had moved to Texas, say, "All men here look as if they were raise in old Kentuky [sic]."

The high mortality rate among the emigrants sent to Texas by the Mainzer Verein during the year 1845–46[19] cannot stand as an indictment against the wholesomeness of the country. Considering the conditions at that time, one is amazed that not more people died. Three thousand persons disembarked without shelter or wood on a marshy coast lacking in drinking

---

[19] The heavy rains during the winter of 1845–1846 made it difficult to move the immigrants from Carlshafen or Indianpoint, as Herff refers to it. Disease broke out, and many died. In a legal action against the Society, a settler, T. H. Florsheim, claims that over 1,000 died at Indianpoint. The official reports admit only 208 deaths there. *Solms-Braunfels Archiv*, LXVIII, 38, 84. See also Biesele, *History of the German Settlements in Texas 1831–1861*, pp. 129–132.

water, having utterly unsuitable, often spoilt food for a period of eight long months—this had to result in utter demoralization because of the hopelessness and poverty. The fact that neither dysentery nor scurvy, so prevalent at that time, have ever broken out epidemically in Texas, before or since, alone proves that it was not the country, but a chain of unfavorable conditions and blunders which caused that mortality upon which the opponents of colonization in Texas rely for argument. I hesitate to say how many would die if one would try to feed 3,000 people on Lake Koshkonong (in Wisconsin) or on the Fox River in the open air on spoilt flour and meal and rancid bacon, on oxen flesh, fish, or turtles without any bread often for days —and this for almost a year. To base one's opinion of the wholesomeness of the climate on such an abnormal situation is as silly as if one were to call Silesia and Poland unhealthy because hundreds succumbed there to hunger and disease during the last famine.[20] In New Braunfels, Fredericksburg, Castroville, on the Mill Creek,[21] and even in the same Indianpoint where three years ago so many died, live thousands of healthy and happy people, who laugh at the folly of those who try to blame a countryside for that caused by the blunders of one society. I have ample opportunity, as a physician, to make comparisons between Texas and Germany with respect to health, and I can decide in favor of the former without any doubt. The open air is, of course, just as healthy here as in Texas, but not

[20] The great Silesian famine reached critical proportions in 1847 following three years of crop failure. Not only was no aid extended to the peasants by the Prussian government, but the censor forbade any publicity on the matter until conditions were so bad they could no longer be hid. Misery and starvation brought on the dreaded hunger-typhus or famine plague, and in certain counties of Silesia the death rate was as high as fifteen to twenty per cent. Not hundreds, but hundreds of thousands succumbed during the famine of 1845–1848. Poultney Bigelow, *History of the German Struggle for Liberty*, IV, 5–12.

[21] Mill Creek is a little stream running through western Austin County. Friedrich Ernst and Charles Fordtran, first German settlers in Texas, settled in the valley of the Mill Creek in 1831, and soon other Germans who had read Ernst's glowing report of the new land followed him and settled in the general area. Industry, first German settlement in Texas, was founded not far from the banks of Mill Creek in 1838, and by 1848, the Mill Creek area was predominantly German, as it still is. Rudolph L. Biesele, *The History of the German Settlements in Texas, 1831–1861*, pp. 43–47.

so the stable-like air of our rooms to which our beloved winter dooms us for such a long time of the year. All those minor ills —colds, coughs, hypochondria, and the like—that embitter the lives of the sick and the physician in this country, are unknown in Texas. There the hereditary enemy of European youth, tuberculosis, is also practically unknown, although the mortality lists of New York, Boston, and Baltimore indicate to us that this terrible disease is as prevalent in those cities as in London.[22]

2) *Cheapness of the land and the basic necessities of life.* In no state of the Union are there more extensive cultivable tracts of land for sale at the Congressional price of $1.25 per acre than in Texas.[23] In any region in the United States where land is offered at this price, it is either uncultivable hilly land or swampland or so distant from any communication system that it is dearer than land which one buys for six times the price in a better location. For one dollar and twenty-five cents one can find land suitable for a settlement in the far West only, where all the difficulties of a northern backwoods life must be endured. These difficulties are, moreover, not inconsiderable and, in dealing with a large number of settlers, almost insurmountable. It is not only the long distance of transporting provisions, but particularly the necessity for a double safeguard against hunger and the disadvantages of a Siberian winter that prove the greatest hindrances to the establishment of an extensive colony and demand enormous operating capital. In Texas these conditions are different. The Congressional price and the minimum acreage purchasable by individuals are fixed by law in all of the other states in the Union except Texas because within the borders of Texas the United States does not own the public lands. The State of Texas has retained these lands in exchange for which it has to bear its own debt burden, created while it was a republic.[24] The low cost of Texas land is further deter-

[22] Herff, in speaking of climate and health, apparently had West Texas in mind throughout. Viktor Bracht, *Texas im Jahre 1848*, pp. 15–31, gives a more complete and more objective report on these points for the whole of Texas, although he also gives a glowing picture of the advantages of the Texas climate.

[23] Public lands of the United States were still at this time being sold at $1.25 per acre under the terms of the basic land law of April 24, 1820.

[24] Section 2 of the Joint Resolution for Annexing Texas to the

mined by the fact that in earlier times these lands were squandered in the most thoughtless manner through the bestowal of land grants, headrights, and gifts to private individuals and companies; which, because of the meager population, do not yet have a market for their surplus lands and would prefer a small sum of cash money to the many thousands of acres of land which are listed under their names on the land rolls of the General Land Office. It is easy to buy whole tracts of ten leagues (one league = 4444 acres[25]) at twenty-five to fifty cents per acre and indeed that in regions not far distant from civilization and suitable for colonization purposes in every respect. Land can be bought even cheaper through the purchase of headrights (that is, title to specified acreages of public lands not yet acquired by private individuals) and carpeting large tracts with them or to acquire the land by having unexpired land grants transferred to oneself even though that way presents difficulties. The cheapness of the purchase price not only makes the land purchase easier financially, but it makes the gain which springs from it—that after colonization individual tracts lying among the settlements might be sold at a high price—so much larger, as well as makes so much surer the repayment of a part of the invested capital to the communities. A striking illustration in this respect has recently been furnished by the tract upon which New Braunfels was founded. This land-complex was bought for twenty-five cents per acre; a part of it was granted to immigrants, and from the portion lying between those plots that was not so granted, not only the whole sum which that entire tract of land originally cost but a considerable amount above this sum was realized through later sales. From that piece of land which was acquired at twenty-five cents per acre, after two years an acre of farmland sold for five dollars, a half-acre townlot for sixty to eighty dollars, and two half-acres

---

United States, passed by Congress on March 1, 1845, and under which Texas was admitted as a State on December 29, 1845, provided that all public lands be retained by Texas and be applied to the payment of the debts and liabilities of the Republic of Texas. After payment of these debts, further lands might be disposed of as Texas might wish. William MacDonald, ed., *Select Documents Illustrative of the History of the United States, 1776–1861* (New York, 1909), 343–345.

[25] Herff's acreage figure is in error. One league is equal to 4428 acres.

provided with water power for 1,200 and 1,400 dollars each, naturally without any improvements through plowing or any other trace of cultivation, but just the virgin forest and prairie-land. Even if such great luck is a rarity, it is conceivable that speculation, based on the scale of lands that have become valuable because of the enveloping civilization, can be successful only where, as in Texas, great complexes can be acquired at a very low price.

The same cheapness prevails with respect to the basic necessities, corn and meat. Where farming requires little labor and cattle-raising none at all, as in Texas, the price of those products conceivably is sure to be very low. The enormous cattle herds that maintain themselves and multiply in the wide marshlands along the Brazos, Galveston Bay, and Matagorda Bay without any human labor furnish a cheap article of food, with the additional advantage that it is easy to transport, or rather, it walks to market by itself. One familiar with the locality who buys at the right time can easily purchase beef in large amounts for one cent and pork for two cents per pound. This cheapness is not only beneficial for acquiring without much expense the sustenance required by the immigrants until the first harvest, but moreover it makes possible the establishment of an easy and effortless source of food and well-being for the colonists through the acquisition of large herds of cattle. Where a cow costs six to ten dollars, a hog two dollars, and sheep and a goat one-half dollar, it is easy to build up large herds, which, if cattle, in the course of nature will be doubled in three years, and if sheep or goats will multiply in far greater progression. All of these purchases of land, as well as of cattle and the like, of course, require persons who know the locality and especially the market conditions.

3) *The great ease with which the necessities of life are obtained from a small quantity of land.* In Iowa or Wisconsin it is impossible for a family to live off the produce of ten *morgen* [a measure of land: one acre equals 1½ morgen]. In those states, corn cannot be raised advantageously,[26] but only wheat and rye. If we compare the yield of both cereal grains with that

---

[26] This statement does not hold up, of course. Iowa particularly and Wisconsin both out-produce Texas in corn. See statistics in *The World Almanac and Book of Facts* of various years.

of corn,[27] we find that an acre produces about twenty-six bushels of wheat or sixteen bushels of rye per bushel of seed; while corn gives a yield of sixty to eighty bushels for one-third of a bushel sown. For the purpose of this comparison I have taken the highest possible yield for wheat and rye but not for corn, disregarding the ravage on the first-named cereal grain by the Hessian fly that quite often causes complete crop failures. A bushel of wheat is worth sixty to seventy cents on the average, a bushel of corn, thirty to forty cents; accordingly the revenue from wheat farming after subtracting the seed would run from $15.00 to $17.30 per acre, while corn would yield from $17.80 to $23.60. In addition, it must be borne in mind that Mexican beans, watermelons, and pumpkins can be grown between the corn without any additional labor save for planting, whereas this is impossible in the case of wheat. If one now assumes the average price of land to be $1.25 per acre in Iowa and Wisconsin and twenty-five to fifty cents per acre in Texas, it is clear that higher-priced land produces less and therefore yields much poorer dividends than the cheap land. The comparison becomes even more one-sided if one compares the work required that in Iowa and Wisconsin is ten times as heavy as in Texas where there are no trees to fell and where all field work can be done during the cool months of the year while in Wisconsin the greater part of it must be done during the summer. Quite apart from these difficulties, *the northern farmer has to use at least half of his land to grow feed for his livestock for the long winters,* whereas the Texas farmer is not bothered either in summer or in winter with the necessity of feeding his livestock. This makes unnecessary the erection of shelters, the work involved in growing and in cutting feed, and giving fodder to the stock; rather it becomes possible whether one has a small or large acreage of land under cultivation or not, to keep as much livestock as one cares to. The countless mountain and valley meadows, which certainly will not be cultivated for a number of decades since there is much better land available

---

[27] Herff uses the term, *Welschkorn*, as well as *Mais*, when referring to corn. The derivation of this term (as given in *Der Grosse Brockhaus*, XX, 157) is interesting. *Korn* is the German word for grain, while one meaning of the term *welsch* is "foreign" (fremdlaendisch), the term having been applied to certain Celtic tribes; thus the name *Welschkorn* ("foreign grain") for American corn.

elsewhere, will furnish for a long time to come a sure means of sustenance not dependent on labor or large landholdings for herds of hundreds and thousands of head of cattle, whose owners need own no more than ten acres of land at the most for cultivation. In New Braunfels, on the Mill Creek, and around Fredericksburg many families live off this amount of land without concern and keep as much livestock as they please. In Wisconsin, on the contrary, there is mostly only woodland grazing in the summertime, with none at all during the winter, and only as much livestock can be kept as grass, clover, oats or rye, and potatoes can be raised for it; and on ten acres, that is not much. The favorable conditions in Texas extend not only to cattle, but also to horses, hogs, sheep, and goats, make possible the pursuit of even more profitable enterprises than cattle-raising, and contribute to the utilization of the advantages cited hereafter, under subtitle number 5,[28] which Texas has over the North.

4) *The slight amount of work required of the colonists and the shorter time between their arrival and their first harvest.* Most of the land destined for cultivation in Texas consists of prairie and so-called mesquite and postoak openings, that is, sparsely covered by mimosa and oak. The labor required of the new colonist that will enable him in the shortest possible time to live off the produce of his fields is therefore extraordinarily slight in comparison with the enormous difficulties which the Northern woods farmer has to overcome. There is no forest to clear in Texas, no underbrush to cut and grub out; rather in most cases only the grassland has to be broken or a few trees which happen to be in the way to be felled and the plow guided around the stumps which are far apart. But far more significant than the mere saving of labor will be the result of it. The settler who wishes to establish a farm in the Northern backwoods must arrive on the spot in the summer in order to build his cabin against the beginning of the severe winter and to prepare at least a part of his land for a future garden or a small pea or potato patch. The cabin of a northern farmer must be built quite differently from that of a southern farmer and requires much more labor if it is to give at least the most neces-

---

[28] The advantage referred to is the possibility of producing in Texas products of greater value than the usual field crops, specifically cotton and wool, and thereby entering the world market.

sary protection against the rigors of the winter. The work necessary to make the field that is to give the first harvest cultivable is heavier than in the South and is even further increased by the longer time consumed in building a house, as well as concern for the cattle that must have at least hay for the winter. Only in rare cases and with the greatest exertion will the woods farmer produce the following summer a harvest sufficient for his needs from the one acre which he can clear and prepare during the first year; thus, in most cases he must be provided with provisions for an additional year. Apart from that, assuming that he makes an adequate first harvest, he still must be supplied with food for at least three months longer before he can become independent than is the case with the immigrant in Texas. If necessary, the Texan can spend the winter without shelter (as was done until the end of February without detriment by our group,[29] who certainly were not accustomed to any hardships) and thus expend all his labor in the field that is to make him independent the following year. He can work in the fields throughout the winter, he does not need to gather feed for his cattle, and, if he arrives at his destination by the end of November, he has sufficient time to make a sure and ample first crop. A simple shelter that will suffice for the winter weather can be erected in four to five days; ten acres of prairie or opening that will give him a fully adequate harvest of corn and sweet potatoes the following August, not to mention the garden vegetables that he will be able to enjoy as pay for his labor by the end of February, can be broken easily in three to four weeks. Thus he requires provisions for only nine months, while the northern farmer has to live out of the sack for at least twelve months and then makes an ample first crop only under very favorable and unusual circumstances. The Texan can keep as many cattle as he wishes the first year, whereas the Northerner will find it difficult enough just to carry his necessary work animals through the six-months-long winter. I believe I can therefore maintain positively that the establishment of a proletariat colony in Wisconsin must cost twice as much as it would cost in Texas, this involving work difficult beyond any description and which in no way returns a wage half-way adequate for the extraordinary exertions during the first year.

[29] That is, the members of the Bettina colony on the Llano River during the winter of 1847–1848.

Let us compare a western woods farmer with an inhabitant of the Texas prairie at the end of the first year. In the first case, we have a dark, damp, and gloomy forest, in the middle of which is a small hedged-in plot where two-feet long upright stumps with sprouted brush roots all over the place show how laborious the struggle against the forest was and how irksome it will continue to be for the next few years. Along with this, one sees a few lean and scrawny cows and a blockhouse, blackened by smoke and inhabited by sallow, dejected-looking faces. Here in Texas we find a simply built frame house with open gallery, a well-cultivated, highly productive piece of land, in the foreground the beautiful green prairie with scattered clumps of trees on the placid hills, in the background cedar brakes or elms and a liveoak thicket, everywhere pretty, fat cattle, and alert, happy people. I am convinced that he who has seen both, as I have, will not long hesitate in his choice of the land where he too would want to build his cabin.

5) *The possibility of producing in Texas products of greater value than the usual field crops and thereby taking part in the world market.* The principal products of the northern free states are foodstuffs, which as long as immigration continues at the present high rate, will find an ever-ready market. If in addition there occur unforeseen circumstances, such as, for example, the Mexican War, the famine of 1847 in Europe,[30] or the California fever,[31] the northern farmer can always be assured of a market for his meal, bacon, and salt meat. Of course, the price of these articles will decrease little by little as more and more are produced; and in those places which are not located on a navigable river, canal, or railroad, it will become so low that it will not pay to transport them to a distant market. In many districts of Illinois, Ohio, and Missouri, this disparity already prevails. I have spoken to emigrants from those states in Texas who have assured me they had been glad to get rid of their wheat at fifteen cents per bushel, their corn at twelve and a half cents per bushel, and their pork at one dollar per barrel (one-half cent per pound). The wealth of those regions will become more and more dependent on industry, as they turn to manufactured products and away from raw products with the exception of metals. Therefore, in the not-too-distant future the

[30] See note 20.
[31] The California gold rush of 1849.

farmer will not be in the most favorable position as he still is at this time, and these disadvantages will continue to increase rather than diminish. Hemp, dye-stuffs, flax, and the like are just those articles which even Europe produces in large amounts, and tobacco remains the only product for the middle states of the Union which will have a greater value in the world market for some time to come. The situation is quite different in Texas, where, in a climate far more favorable to northerners than that of the southern states of the Union, the products of that Southland that constantly maintain a high value in trade, yea, will ever attain a higher value, can be produced. Because of the decrease in the annual rate of production in the West Indies, cotton and sugar will probably go up in price. The present low price of these products cannot be regarded as normal, since it was caused by the extraordinary conditions in Europe and is therefore to be regarded as conditional and transitory. In proportion to their weight, both products have a much higher intrinsic value than the raw products of the North, thus making it profitable for those producers situated a long way from the market to transport those products.

The argument, heard here and there, that it is impossible to produce those products without slaves, has absolutely no basis in the case of cotton and in the case of sugar only conditionally so. Cotton requires exactly the same labor as corn and is raised on the Mill Creek with profit and without the least detriment to their health by hundreds of Germans who neither own nor lease Negroes. In the cultivation of sugar cane, the field work is not more difficult than in the case of corn, but the regions which are especially suited to the production of sugar cane are usually not healthy; moreover, cane cultivation requires a very large operating capital for the installation of boiling-houses and sugar mills, thus in a colony of penniless persons it can be considered only insofar as it avails them of the possibility to earn some money as day laborers.

On the other hand, cotton very easily may be grown on a small scale and will remain for a long time to come as good as cash money, since it is always a sought-after article on the world market. However, the production of wool offers the Texas farmer even greater opportunities for profit. No country in the world, with the possible exception of Spain and Australia, is more suited to the pursuit of this important division of husbandry. The dry mountain pastures, rich in nutritive vegetation, provide wholesome food in summer and winter; there is a surplus of pure flowing water for the purpose of wool-cleaning; and the climate that is more dry than damp is usually advantageous to the health of the herds. No part of the United States, not even West Virginia and the mountain districts of Georgia, offers similar advantages for the extensive and almost effortless pursuit of sheep-raising. The only work consists of herding and shearing. Nursing and feeding are not necessary, and one therefore needs only the tenth part of the shepherds required for a certain number of sheep in the northern regions. Moreover, the sheep of neighboring Mexico, if they are bought in large numbers by men who know their business, are extraordinarily cheap. These can be had in lots of a thousand at 25 cents to 40 cents (37 and 60 *kreuzers*) per head. To be sure, the wool is not of the better sort but, through cross-breeding with higher-bred rams, is easily improved, as has already been profitably done by one of the German farmers on the upper Guadalupe, Herr von Behr.[32] At least half of the wool market in the United States is still supplied from outside sources; thus, the outlook for a market outlet for Texas wool appears very favorable. The raising of cotton, wool, and similar products greatly moderates the weight of the chief criticism which the opponents of Texas level against this land. This criticism is the present deficiency in waterways; I say present, because in the not-too-distant future, the streambeds of the Brazos and Colorado, along with the Guadalupe—all rivers which in volume of water are fully equal to the Main and Neckar—will be so regulated that the disadvantage will also be completely removed. Land transport by wagon, it is true, is much more expensive,

---

[32] Ottomar von Behr was one of a number of highly educated men who came to Texas following the revolution of 1848 in Germany. He built his home on the western banks of the Guadalupe River, west of New Braunfels, where, after other men of culture joined him, the settlement of Sisterdale, the so-called "Latin Settlement," was founded. Moritz Tiling, *History of the German Element in Texas* . . . (Houston, 1913), 122–123. Ottomar von Behr wrote a book called *Good Advice for Emigrants to the United States with Special Reference to Texas*, in which he gives practical advice for farmers and craftsmen and on the title page of which he calls himself a practical farmer. This book was published in 1847 in Leipzig and was perhaps the source of Herff's information. Biesele, *History of the German Settlements in Texas, 1831–1861*, p. 171n.

but it still amounts to a much smaller percentage considering the intrinsic value of the things to be transported than in the case of the raw products of the North, meal and meats, which in relation to their importance are of little monetary value. An example may illustrate this. The freight on a barrel of flour, weighing about two hundred pounds[33] and worth four dollars, amounts to about twenty-five cents from an interior town of Illinois down the Illinois River to St. Louis; thus, on a hundred pounds of flour worth two dollars, the freight is twelve and one-half cents, which comes to six and one-half[34] per cent. Freight on a hundred-weight of wood from New Braunfels to Indianpoint on the sea in Texas is one dollar, which is five per cent in a value of twenty dollars, while Illinois flour is carried to a river port [St. Louis] which is more than eighteen hundred miles from the state's real harbor, New Orleans. I have figured the price of flour as it is in St. Louis and not as it is in Illinois, while I figured the price of wool as that which the producer can get at any time, which makes the situation in favor of Texas even more advantageous. To be sure, anyone transporting bricks or corn by wagon out of the interior of Texas to a seaport will not earn much.

6) *Texas has up to now been the only region where a grandiose colonizing undertaking has been accomplished and has succeeded at least to the extent that large districts have been cultivated, towns founded in the wilderness, and thousands of Germans guided to an independent and happy station in life.* If one compares the German settlements in Texas with those in Missouri, Illinois, and other states, a significant difference is immediately apparent. In the first state, immigration was concentrated in large numbers upon an appointed place and was regulated according to an organized plan, whereas in the whole of the rest of America it was only in exceptional cases and only on a very small scale that any centralization or any actual colonization out of Europe took place. Usually the family remaining behind answered the call of their American relatives to those regions or the hometown neighbor that of his former

---

[33] Herff here uses the term *Centner*, which is the metric hundredweight (110.23 pounds) in use on the Continent, but he has in mind the short American hundred-weight (100 pounds).

[34] Six and one-half is the percentage given in the original text; it should be six and one-quarter per cent.

countryman or, particularly the German, the universal report of the excellence of the new homeland. Scattered groups of German settlements arose as a result of chance, without an overall purpose, without organization, every man depending on his own strength or his own money, without any assistance in provisions, means of transportation, or farm implements, such as the Adelsverein has done in Texas for more than four years under the greatest variety of conditions and with the greatest obstacles. The entire course of development which the colonization of Texas has taken is diametrically different from that which transformed the far west of the North-American Union into states. The experience of twenty-five years has constituted in Texas a school for regulated, concentrated immigration whose sum of good and bad experiences has become the blood and sinew of every inhabitant of the land, whereas in the North such a school of experience is yet to be built, and all costly experiences, all vicissitudes which in Texas one has learned to know and to avoid, must be suffered anew. In the northern part of the Union, the individual squatter, half-hunter and half-farmer, moves far out from civilization with his family and builds his hut and clears his field, unconcerned about paying for the land upon which he dwells. This among others is the chief reason why in the Union it is not possible, not even in the most distant wilderness, to buy an extensive, continuous tract of land at the Congressional price, since the fairest tracts have for years already been appropriated by squatters, who have the pre-emptory right to purchase at $1.25 per acre a right which they will sell only at a high price or will exercise themselves by claiming the fairest tracts when civilization catches up with them. The squatter is usually followed by the first colonist, equally solitary, and finally towns are established when the market demand has attracted merchants, speculators, and craftsmen. It is quite different in Texas. There are no squatters there in the American sense and never have been.

The large number of powerful Indian tribes and later the insecurities caused by the war with Mexico made it necessary that towns were established before farms were laid out. Long before the Anglo-Americans occupied the land, the Spaniards followed a similar colonization policy, and, in the towns of San Antonio, Goliad, and Nacogdoches, which a hundred years ago lay completely isolated in a wilderness inhabited by thieving and murderous Indians, one can still see evidences of that policy. To be sure, the motives for settlement here were different than in the northern part of the Union. The extension of Catholicism and the thirst for gold drove those bold adventurers, those old conquistadores, in the first few decades after the discovery of the new continent from the cleft of the La Raja[35] to the mouth of the Ohio, and all the settlements that were established came about as a result of one or the other of these two motives. Thus, in the midst of the snowy reaches of the Cordilleras, towns that could be reached only by llamas or donkeys were founded in order that the riches of the neighboring mountains could be exploited; in the middle of the primeval forest surrounded by numerous Indian tribes there arose mission towns and fortified monasteries, the ruins of which still are found frequently in the most distant districts of Texas and from which armed groups of missionaries went out in the cause of the holy church. The Anglo-Americans operated otherwise. Their towns were laid out along the best trade routes and in the regions most fertile and rich in the products of agriculture and industry. In the Union the town arises with the market; in Texas, on the other hand, it had to be just the opposite because of the previously mentioned necessity for having the protection of a community. A compact, courageous, and intelligent population first of all had to drive away the Indians and then to disperse themselves to cultivate the neighborhood that had been made secure. Practically all developments in Texas were directed accordingly, and the experience of twenty-five years has removed the difficulties that in the beginning made so arduous the establishment of concentrated settlements in the midst of the wilderness and their provision from a great distance during the first year.

Colonization still follows the same pattern except for the modifications which stable political conditions, particularly the annexation to the mighty Union, have brought about. Around the farthest settlements is drawn a cordon of well-mounted and well-armed border troops (Texian Rangers), who are acquainted with the conduct of war against the Indians and count among their ranks Indian scouts (spies) from friendly tribes. Every thirty English miles a company is garrisoned in a well-fortified

---

[35] The Continental Divide.

camp, and its only occupation is to make sure that no Indian crosses over the restraining border without a pass from the governor. It is almost impossible that a small party of Indians, much less larger bodies, elude the watchfulness of those troops and get within this line that stretches from the Rio Grande through points on the middle Nueces, the Cañon de Uvalde, the upper Medina, the Llano, and Sandy Creek, to the Red River Tradinghouse.[36] The security of the settlers against raids is certainly greater than in the western stations of Iowa where until just recently Black Hawk's now dispersed warriors held sway. The new settlements of the Texas frontier regions are being made beyond this military line by large numbers of well-armed men leading a semi-military life, who, because of their imposing numbers and fortified dwellings, force the unwilling Indians to move westward after a short time. If the settlement succeeds, that is, if it makes an abundant first-year harvest or if the colonists are able to provision themselves in order to maintain themselves a second year, the border cordon moves forward, and under its protection individual farms come into being which are often twenty miles distant from the nearest neighbor yet are more secure than a lonely farm in the Fichtel Mountains[37] or even a village in Abruzzi.[38] In this fashion were founded the towns of New Braunfels, Fredericksburg, and the settlements on the Llano, for which our society laid the groundwork. The whole course of the history of Texas colonization in a certain measure has prepared for a regulated large-scale colonization and facilitates such an undertaking in an extraordinary manner, in that the avoidance and alleviation of the difficulties connected with such planned enterprises has been learned. To a far greater extent, however, an undertaking which existed for several years in Texas has prepared the way for the establishment of a national colony for the relief of the

---

[36] Most probably Coffee's Trading Post, which was established by Colonel Holland Coffee in 1834 on the Red River in what is now Grayson County. See Bright Ray, *Legends of the Red River Valley* (San Antonio, 1941), 191–199.

[37] A mountain group of Bavaria, thickly wooded, and having a raw and damp climate.

[38] A group of provinces in the mountainous section of south central Italy. Population is sparse because of the hard climate in the snow-covered Appenines. *Der Grosse Brockhaus*, I (Leipzig, 1928), 47–48.

proletariat. This was the former Mainzer Verein, the first and up to now the only organization that in its own way has as its purpose to lead large groups of Germans to an uninhabited region far removed from the supporting sources of an advanced culture and actively through a local and transatlantic board of management to direct and govern; at least, that was the intention. Although many results of this undertaking admittedly cannot be characterized as successful and gratifying, the question of the possibility of colonizing *en masse*, particularly the question of the transatlantic leadership of those colonists, nevertheless has in the main been unquestionably answered by this achievement.

The transportation of numerous proletarians without cost to them and their present prosperous existence in their new homeland made possible by a not-too-costly support prior to their first harvest already makes the undertaking of the Mainzer Verein quite similar to the projected national enterprise. If, in the meantime, those gentlemen, through honest liquidation of their obligations in Texas, which amounts to about $150,000,[39] have secured their land-holdings by grant, many a point of contact might be offered for a national colonization project with the earlier work that came to a halt shortly before the final goal was achieved. Much more important than the results achieved by the Verein, the sum total of the experiences undergone will once again tip the balance in favor of Texas. The Verein has in numerous instances shown how, but oftener how not, to go about accomplishing a colonization project. One finds in Texas that not only the officials of the Verein, who paid heavily for experience, but also all of the six thousand Germans which the Verein sent over went to that school of experience and know the answers, bought with the sweat of much lost labor, to problems which will arise out of the intended undertaking. All of the inhabitants can be relied upon concerning the smallest details of Texas frontier life and the minutest particulars of the

---

[39] This debt, contracted in Texas by the Society, evoked criticism and attack in the Texas press. The fact it could not be repaid out of the capital of the Society was the chief reason for the Society's failure to attain the goal it had set. Hermann Spiess, commissioner-general of the Society, replying on October 28, 1847, to such an attack in the press, blamed unforeseen expenses and the disturbed European conditions for the deficit. Biesele, *History of the German Settlements in Texas, 1831–1861*, pp. 158–159n.

provision and transportation questions and, with their great interest in the success of national colonization, are to be regarded as a well-organized corps of effective fellow-workers. Of no little importance, moreover, is the fact that perhaps in no other section of North America is there a greater number of educated and talented Germans than in Texas. Already during the era of the Republic many men who were not motivated by distress but by some idea streamed into that new Icaria,[40] as our society was referred to recently by an ill-advised newspaper writer. The Adelsverein likewise took a large number of cultured men overseas because such a seemingly grandiose undertaking promised much. Indeed, it is a comforting experience to meet, often in the heart of the Indian country, so many talented and cultured countrymen who are distinguished not only from the social standpoint but also in the field of learning. Excellent physicians and able scientists of German extraction are found in surprising numbers, even including notables (such as Baumgarten[41] of Clausthal, former editor of the *Surgical Almanac*, and Lindheimer,[42] the botanist). Once the first material problems have been solved, the thirst for culture is observable; singing societies, reading societies, and schools have been founded in all German towns, and the college (for which the government has allotted 4,444 acres of land as an endowment) will soon be more than merely a name.[43]

[40] From the Utopian novel by Etienne Cabet, *A Voyage to Icaria*. Followers of Cabet, a French "communist" writer during the 1848 revolution, dreamed of migrating from a decayed Europe to a new Icaria in the virgin soil of Texas and there setting up an earthly paradise of liberty and equality with their leader as dictator. They were not revolutionaries, but preached patience and nonviolence. Max Nomad, *Apostles of Revolution* (Boston, 1939), 29–30. See also note 71.

[41] Dr. Baumgarten came to Texas in 1847 upon assurance of receiving a grant of land from the Society. He had been serving as an army surgeon in Brunswick just prior to coming to Texas. *Solms-Braunfels Archiv*, XVII, 286; XXVII, 19, 20.

[42] Dr. Ferdinand Jacob Lindheimer, besides being a botanist, was also the first editor of the *Neu Braunfelser Zeitung*. He studied law in Germany, became a liberal politically, and had to flee to the United States in 1833, coming to Texas in 1836 in time to take part in the Revolution. Biesele, *History of the German Settlements in Texas, 1831–1861*, p. 224n.

[43] Upon petition of residents of Austin County, Hermann's University was incorporated by the Republic of Texas on January 27, 1844, and a league of land (4,428 acres, rather than 4,444) was

Whether the progress of those cultural endeavors will lead to an improved nationality freed of many harmful appendages, or whether it will promote a blending with the Anglo-American race, time will tell. The maintenance of the total or undivided German nationality is in my opinion neither possible nor desirable so long as it does not offer anything better than the freedom and the well-being of the individual which through the years the Anglo-American has offered.

Not only in purely scholarly lines but precisely in the field of colonization does one find in Texas a school of able men who have been tried by severe and laboriously obtained experience. He who compares the achievements of the prominent officials over there (Prince Solms, Meusebach, Spiess, Dresel, Bene)[44] with the available means, the obstructions in the way, and the newness of the undertaking will agree with me in this contention. Show me a land that in this respect surpasses Texas, which has to offer in addition to rich material resources such an intellectually able and practically trained cadre for a national undertaking on a larger scale. That spirit, and this is no unimportant matter, will permeate the raw transplanted masses and will further the execution of the main objective more than will any financial means.

After these admittedly somewhat copious introductory remarks, which nevertheless are necessary as a preface to many points in the following exposition, I commence the actual

---

donated to it by the Congress of Texas. A two-story building was after several years erected at Frelsburg, but no classes were ever held in it. By the time of the Civil War, the "University" was still a dream, and remained so. *Ibid.*, 215–216.

[44] Prince Carl of Solms-Braunfels arrived in Texas on November 22, 1844, as the first commissioner-general of the Society in Texas and was instrumental in the founding of New Braunfels. He was succeeded in early 1845 by Baron von Meusebach, who arrived in May. Meusebach founded Fredericksburg, Castell, and Leiningen, and made the famous treaty of 1847 with the Comanche Indians. Hermann Spiess, along with Herff one of the founders of the Bettina colony, became commissioner-general in July, 1847. Gustav Dresel, who accompanied Spiess and Herff in advance of the Bettina colonists, was appointed general business agent to try to clear up the Society's financial affairs, but he failed in the attempt. Louis Bene succeeded Spiess as commissioner-general in 1848, the last official to hold that office in Texas. He returned to Germany in 1852. See Biesele, *History of the German Settlements in Texas, 1831–1861*, 123, 158–159.

sketch for a proletariat colony in Texas. It is inherent in the nature of things that before a definite operational basis to regulate the actual work of execution is established, no well-rounded, completely worked out, and suitable proposal for that important question can be put forth. It must suffice, therefore, to lay down certain guiding principles and to verify certain special points with statistics.

1) Acquisition of the Land

The most suitable location is the northwestern part of Texas, that portion of the country lying between the Colorado and Rio Grande del Norte, beginning at a distance of 25 to 40 miles from the sea, extending to the sources of the Colorado, the Nueces, and the Guadalupe, and to the foothills of the easternmost ranges of the Sierra Madre. An area as large as the state of Illinois, the greater part is well suited for agriculture and the whole well adapted for the raising of cattle, horses, and sheep. All the advantages of Texas set forth in the previous paragraphs have a special degree of validity as regards this part of the country. Especially suitable locations could be designated on the upper Medina, the upper Nueces, the Cañon de Uvalde 60 miles from San Antonio, the upper Cibolo, the country between New Braunfels and Seguin, the upper Guadalupe, the Pedernales River, the upper San Marcos, the Rio Blanco, the Little River and Brush Creek, the upper Colorado, the Sandy Creek, the San Saba, Brady Creek, the Concho River, and the upper Coleto.[45] In all of these places are great, continuous stretches of good land to be had at a most reasonable cost. There are three methods of effecting this acquisition:

1) *Through purchase from private individuals.* This is the safest but at the same time most expensive method of acquisition. On the average, however, one can still count on a price of 35 cents to 75 cents per acre for large tracts of land in the more distant parts of the country, as on the upper Pedernales, around the mouth of the San Saba, along the upper Medina, and the Cañon de Uvalde; lands which are in the secure and legally

[45] The Coleto, which flows into the Guadalupe River south of Victoria, seems to be out of place in this grouping of streams. It is not in the area that Herff had in mind for colonization purposes. Numerous English and Spanish names are misspelled in the original text, and it is probable that Herff had some other river in mind, perhaps the North Concho.

guaranteed possession of private individuals; and where the proportion of cultivable land to woodland or pasture is throughout a very favorable one, that is, at least three-fourths. It is quite easy for an experienced man to investigate the validity of land titles in Texas and to be guided accordingly in the purchase of lands. In general, the oldest titles, namely, the Spanish and Mexican, are the best; the most questionable are those which were bestowed during the early days of the Republic of Texas under the name of "league and labor,"[46] and which are inscribed with the notation, "not recommendable," by the traveling board of land commissioners. These titles are unencumbered by surveying fees.

2) *Through acquisition of headrights.* This term designates those titles to certain quotas of lands, given for service in war or for any other reason, which the recipient may have surveyed for himself at some favored location still in the possession of the government and outside any other grant. As a whole, this method of acquisition is not especially advisable, for not much government land suitable for cultivation and for extensive colonization is left within the regions I designated as preferable. Also the surveying costs of such scattered buying of headrights are rather considerable, so that the resulting apparent advantage of cheap acquisition is thereby pushed into the background. One can buy now and then, to be sure, a Texas headright (that is, one granted by the old Republic or the Mexican government) of 640 acres for 70 dollars or nine cents per acre;[47] the surveying alone will come to 42 dollars; a total, therefore, of sixteen cents per acre,[48] which, taking into consideration the great distance of such lands as well as the difficulty of acquiring in this manner suitable contiguous lands, is too much money.

[46] Under the terms of the imperial Mexican colonization law of January 4, 1823, no fewer than one labor (177 acres) was given to each farmer, and no fewer than one league (4,428 acres) to each stockfarmer. H. Yoakum, *History of Texas*, I (Austin, 1935), 217. These land grants were recognized by the Republic of Texas. Naturally, settlers represented themselves as both farmers and stockfarmers and thereby received a grant of a "league and labor" as headrights.

[47] The calculation is erroneous here. 640 acres divided into 70 dollars comes to almost eleven cents per acre.

[48] Here again, the correct approximate rate is eighteen cents per acre.

3) *Through acquisition of a government grant.* By such a grant is meant a certain area of land conferred by the government upon a private individual or corporation under the condition that a certain number of immigrants be settled thereon. Since the annexation of Texas by the Union, no further grants are being made; therefore, strictly speaking, this method is out of the question. But there still exist at this time government grants formerly made, additions to which might be negotiated for a reasonable stipulation as soon as the holders of these have satisfactorily executed the legal conditions of their acquisition. This is true in the case of the holders of the former Castro and Fisher-Miller grants. Because of the complete lack of relatively important streams, the former can scarcely be recommended; nor do I know enough concerning the circumstances of the title rights, which have never been contested, to give an accurate report thereon. The latter, however, offers from a physical, climatic, and commercial viewpoint the greatest advantages of all the inland districts of West Texas. These advantages will become still greater because the grantee, through the previous activity of the Mainzer Verein, will fall heir to a proven, still active (though now rather slow) enterprise, the existence or nonexistence of which for the last five years has been an important question for all of West Texas. Concerning the legal status of the property (if one can call by the name of property a mortgaged property whose ownership is still dependent on partly unfulfilled stipulations), I believe I can give the most satisfactory information. For the present, that fair tract of land is by no means the free and disposable property of the Mainzer Verein, but one can say with certainty that it will be as soon as that society will have paid off the considerable debt of 140-150,000 dollars still outstanding, mainly in West Texas. As soon as certain guarantees of payment are assured, the government of Texas will grant the undertaking every possible assistance as well as any possible remission of earlier unfulfilled terms. This will certainly be the case when the probability is established that this work of colonization that is in every respect so extremely profitable to Texas will be continued and completed. However, as yet (since the debts have in no wise been paid), not a clod of these fair lands can be acquired from the Society, and the circumstance that occasionally sales of this

kind are made[49] can be attributed only to the lack of accurate instruction in their own affairs which prevails among the European management. It is my duty to call upon everyone who has any influence among the members of this undertaking that was so nobly begun and perhaps to be so lamentably terminated to assert that influence and to exert every effort to prevail upon the shareholders, who surely want to do the right thing, to use the only means which is not only honorable but also supported by justice to complete the job equitably and with the least possible loss. No one would more willingly do justice to the aims of the founders, no one knows better the ofttimes selfish reasons for so many blundering actions undertaken against the will of the majority, than I. It would be a great pity, not only for the millions thrown away but also for the whole sum of honor and talent, which were at least as much a part of the cause as not; it would be a great pity if the total of the experiences and the strenuous preparatory labors were to come to nought, if this enterprise founded by some of the most distinguished men of Germany were to die a disgraceful death.

It would indeed be desirable if some national enterprise could become associated with this older work. As far as I know, action to undertake such a project again was being seriously considered by the ministry of one of the large German states prior to the March revolution of 1848, and it would be advisable to go further into the plan. To be sure, the terms of purchase that the former holder (the Verein) would allow the new enterprise, a national colony, would have to be most favorable, and the cost per acre, inclusive of the partly paid surveying cost, could not be higher than forty cents at the most. As is self-evident, in the choice of a site for colonization purposes, what must be kept in mind are the basic considerations for the success of such an undertaking, health, fertility, an adequate wood and water supply, and above all a site favorable for the extensive raising of cattle. It is therefore desirable that the site of the

---

[49] Louis Bene authorized Gustav Dresel to sell Nassau Farm, a league of land in Fayette County which was the first tract of land acquired by the Society in 1843. The tract was sold in 1848 to Otto von Roeder for $14,000 in order to alleviate the pressure from outstanding obligations of the Society. Biesele, *History of the German Settlements in Texas, 1831–1861*, 158–159n.

colony be bordered by lands suitable for cattle raising, though not suitable for cultivation. The colonists would thus have sufficient pasture for their cattle without the necessity of the colony buying the pasturelands, because [the lands] would never be shut off by enclosures since they are unsuited for cultivation.

In the choice of a site for a town, particular heed must be paid to the proximity of natural trade routes, as well as to any waterpower potential within the colony. The latter point is important not only because of the necessity of installing saw- and grist-mills, but also in regard to the possibility of manufacturing in certain lines. The State of Mexico, which has a surplus of precious metals and other raw materials, is, because of the lack of skills and illiteracy of most of its inhabitants, handicapped in the development of industry and receives practically all of her manufactured goods from outside of the country. The influx of these foreign products is along two great channels of overland commerce, by sea or by land via Vera Cruz, and via Santa Fe in New Mexico. The trade through Vera Cruz is mainly, almost wholly, with the southern sections of Mexico, namely, the provinces immediately surrounding the capital of the country. From this section, in earlier times, commerce was carried by muletrain with great difficulty along impracticable trails, made unsafe by robbers and Indians, to the more northerly provinces in the wider part of Mexico: Durango, Nuevo Leon, Chihuahua, Coahuila, and New Mexico. Only since the end of Spanish rule in Mexico has the trade originated on land, whereby in exchange for their gold and silver bullion, the latter provinces have been able to acquire their wares over a shorter and less dangerous route from the United States.

For a number of years this so-called Santa Fe trade has been carried on with extraordinary profit out of the State of Missouri by means of large, specially equipped caravans, and has been all the more profitable since it has been possible in these northern provinces for the most part, to evade the duties levied on the trade through Vera Cruz. The caravan trail ran from Independence, Missouri, via the western tributaries of the Arkansas to the headwaters of the Red and Rio Grande rivers. Because of the great distance and the lack of water on the High Plains, the trip was extraordinarily strenuous and time-consuming. The most staple commodities were fancy-goods and coarse cotton textiles, for which Santa Fe actually was only the wholesale distribution point, the goods being retailed to consumers by the merchants of the more prosperous middle provinces of Chihuahua, Coahuila, Durango, and others. One can imagine how lucrative the Santa Fe trade must be to induce whole caravans, which depart yearly from Independence, to undertake the dangerous and difficult journey. Since the annexation of Texas by the Union, however, men have pondered ways and means of shortening the roundabout route, thereby decreasing the considerable costs of land transport. The much shorter distance between the Texas cities of San Antonio, Austin, and New Braunfels and the actual market of the Santa Fe trade in Chihuahua could be turned to advantage and thus not only save time, but also carry on direct trade without the Santa Fe middleman. Shipments of goods from the United States are dispatched from New Orleans to Lavaca, Corpus Christi, or Brownsville on the Rio Grande in two to four days; from thence to Chihuahua is a distance of only 560 to 600 miles and part of that distance is through settlements (for 250 English miles), the other part through well-watered and, with some construction, easily passable terrain, whereas the trail from Independence to Santa Fe will come to at least 1,800 English miles, a distance inhabited only by Indians and buffaloes and, for the greater part, only a woodless and waterless steppe. Shortly before my departure, Colonel Hays, the well-known conqueror of the Mexican guerillas in the last war, first traversed this shorter route with a caravan of 80 men and brought back most favorable reports of his expedition, so that one can be quite certain that all gains which in the past accrued to Missouri will now be available to Texas, particularly West Texas. To further increase these advantages, it is necessary to produce a part of the most marketable commodities, namely, cotton fabrics, rough woolen blankets, and the like, within the country (Texas). For this reason, it is essential to procure for the planned colony sufficient natural waterpower necessary for spinning and weaving mills. The great value of the site of the town of New Braunfels is based primarily on this consideration. A group of Virginians, headed by a certain Mr. Merryweather,[50]

---

[50] The Society records show that in March of 1847, W. H. Meriwether owned three city lots in the town of New Braunfels. *Solms-Braunfels Archiv*, XLIX, 61. In 1860, he was the owner of grist and

one of the wealthiest men of that state who has also resided for a number of years in Europe, especially in England and Italy, has in mind the establishment of extensive cotton and wool manufacturing for the Chihuahua trade in that town, which has a tremendous waterpower potential because of the unvarying flow of the Comal River.[51] Since both raw products can be produced in abundance in the immediate surroundings, the price of land in this neighborhood has conceivably increased rapidly, as I have heretofore indicated. Exactly the same conditions pertain to the choice of a similar site in the San Saba or upper Medina River regions and will be of continuing benefit in the projected development of those lands, namely, town sites not allotted to immigrants.

2) Distribution of the Land

The acquired land has to fulfill two purposes:

a) to give the transplanted proletarians the opportunity through the labor of their hands to become independent and respected persons;

b) to furnish the means to cover partly at least the costs of the undertaking.

The first purpose will be fulfilled by the fact that the different families will be given the opportunity, with sufficient aid in the form of provisions, tools, and especially energetic direction and organization of their work, to produce their first crop at the right time on their allotted acreage, so that they cannot only stand upon their own feet after the first year but after a while bring in a profit. There can be no thought of any repayment, based on each family's share of the total cost, as is envisaged in the Kunzel Plan.[52] In Texas one is indeed easily able to earn

---

sawmills in New Braunfels. Biesele, *History of the German Settlements in Texas, 1831–1861*, p. 138.

[51] The Comal River, which begins and ends within the city limits of present-day New Braunfels, is fed from the largest spring in the State of Texas. Its flow varies only some twelve and one-half per cent from average throughout the year according to the *Texas Almanac, 1945–1946*, pp. 435, 548.

[52] Dr. Heinrich Kunzel, one of the editors of *Der deutsche Auswanderer*, a German weekly published in Darmstadt in 1847, was a vociferous critic of the Society. He was also a member of the National Society for German Emigration and Colonization. His plan called for colonization elsewhere than Texas. *Solms-Braunfels Archiv*, LXVIII, 8, 68ff, 85.

several hundred guilders along with his usual necessities of life on a plot of ten acres, whereas in Iowa, because of the lower value of the produce and the difficulties of stock-farming, this would not be the case. But who will want to collect the purchase price after ten years; who will want to bear the high court costs which in the United States anyone who brings suit against the actual occupier of the land is subject to? Not too much can be expected of the honesty of the proletarian, since he is in the habit of looking upon a loan and a gift as identical, and he will soon learn that in America it is wiser to relinquish a claim on a trifle, of which he is not the actual possessor, than to institute legal proceedings for its recovery which might cost twenty times what it is worth. He knows, therefore, that the colonization society will not contest the possession of a few acres, though they hold a mortgage on it. Even if by going to court the society would try to collect the many thousand claims of several hundred guilders against the occupiers of these mortgaged tracts, it would soon realize that, added to the sums which it has already expended in behalf of the colonists, it would have to sink a ten-times greater sum into the bottomless moneybags of the lawyers and even then it would be difficult to realize its objective. As a rule, the jury, which always in such cases favors the poor, will likewise do so in this case under the least pretext of right, which it will not be difficult to show is on the side of the proletarian because of many an unfulfilled even though small obligation on the part of the society. Even here in Europe, with its thousand-year-old minutely detailed code of laws and court procedures, it might not be advisable to sign such a contract and base a colonization scheme upon its fulfillment. The immense complications of accounting and central administration inherent in such a procedure alone could prove to present difficulties sufficient to cause the total failure of the procedure. Therefore, ways and means must be considered to arrange for payment of the heavy expenses for which the enterprisers of a large-scale colonization will be subject to in some other manner than by payment on the part of the colonists. This can be done partly through the realization of the advantages already mentioned which accrue to the remaining citizens of having the impoverished members of the community leave, that is to say: the alleviation of the burden of the poor and the enlargement of community property through the escheated property of those who have left. On the other hand, however, this must be brought about by the practical use of certain tracts of lands that are not allotted to settlers but retained by the society, and that will increase in value because of the development of the colony. I have demonstrated by the example of New Braunfels how rapidly raw land in the neighborhood of a new settlement that offers mercantile and manufacturing advantages will increase in value. Particular care must therefore be taken by the transatlantic leadership of the enterprise that such sites within the colony be reserved for the corporate body. Advantageous townsites must not only be reserved, but the town must immediately be laid out. It is particularly desirable to induce some wealthier persons through the free distribution of some of the townlots and other inducements to settle here and thus soon to bring the new place *en vogue*. Waterpower sites, mill sites, and districts covered with fine craftwoods, building lumber, and shingle lumber must be reserved as long as possible, and if the society itself will not use these sites in establishing large commercial enterprises, their sale should be deferred until the time of highest prosperity of the colony.

During the first two years, when needy settlers will raise products mostly for their own livelihood and less so for market, the influx of well-to-do persons will not be particularly heavy. Still, many a wealthy German might persuade himself to settle in the new colony even during the first few unremunerative years because of the presence of his own countrymen and their large labor power; and just such people, who quite apart from their financial strength will be able to impart to the uneducated masses the benefits of knowledge and culture, must be attracted here through the assurance of certain benefits. Another source of reimbursement of monetary outlay will be realized by the colonization society through the skillful employment of the trade and industrial advantages which will soon become apparent in the newly established colony. By being at the same time a trading company, if this society will grasp how to utilize the wool and cotton market which has been created by their settlers; if, because of its preponderant capital and superior knowledge of local conditions, it will secure for itself a sort of monopoly over these profitable products against which there can be little competition; if it will utilize water power within its territories for the establishment of factories; if, finally, it will secure for itself a large part of the trade with Mexico, then there will have to be great gain from the venture proportionate to the very considerable expenditures.

Undoubtedly it is necessary not only for the protégés, but also for the participating members of the society that the society be incorporated and thus be an officially recognized and authorized legal body in its relations with the American government and public. As regards the last-named activity in the field of trade and industry,[53] it would be of infinite value if permission could be obtained from the government to establish a bank. In Texas, however, the establishment of such institutions, which are of extraordinary importance to all enterprises based on shareholdings, is at the present time forbidden.[54] On the other hand, an institution of this sort could easily be established in Louisiana and through proper financial management result in success for those taking part in the venture. Almost all American banks are founded on the basis of some construction or trade enterprise—for instance, a railroad, a canal, a new town development, or other such—and few have a more promising foundation than a bank, established under the auspices of the colonization society and projected upon the prospects of the gain from the wool market and the Chihuahua trade in certain manufactured commodities. I am sure I do not have to mention the fact that in the incorporation of every company, including establishing a bank, those persons who function as authorized agents of the enterprise must be American citizens.

3) Actual Colonization

The mere distribution of a certain quantity of land to impoverished colonists is just as useless and helps the critical condition of the large numbers of the proletariat sent to America without means just as little as do these benevolent societies that restrict their benevolence to advice. The task of a coloniza-

---

[53] That is, the securing of a partial monopoly of the projected Mexican trade.

[54] Section 30, Article VII of the Constitution of 1845, states: "No corporate body shall hereafter be created, renewed, or extended, with banking or discounting privileges." John Sayles, ed. *The Constitutions of the State of Texas, with the Reconstruction Acts of Congress, the Constitution of the Confederate States and of the United States*, 211.

tion society wishing to fulfill its purpose is rather to bring about this miracle through the proper support of their protégés. This obligation will be discharged:
1) Through sending the emigrants to the colony at the right season of the year.
2) Through furnishing them with provisions until the first harvest.
3) Through providing the necessary field and building tools.
4) Through conducting the kind of leadership of the emigrants which knows how to institute the regulations necessary to the attainment of the main purpose, the independence of the colonists after the first year, and to execute these regulations earnestly and energetically.

The expenditures necessary in the first three points are those spent for actual purchases and for wages for the different kinds of labor engaged therein. These would be considerable and would require a disproportionately, practically unattainable capital. This capital would be difficult to replace on the part of the society by means of the expedients listed in the previous section unless the greater part of the necessary purchases as well as practically the whole of the expense budget for human labor could be directed toward those purposes by the labor-power of the colonists. The society gives the colonist the means to assure himself an independent livelihood, it guarantees him a certain quota of land, it undertakes his transportation, it furnishes him with tools and provisions; therefore, it also has an established claim upon his labor-power and certainly the more so the less this is used for the profit of the society rather than for promoting the benevolent goal which it has set for itself. Were the concern here merely a moral obligation, because of the requirements of equitable claims the society would get the worst of it in its relations with most of the proletariat. Generally speaking, very few would work for the common purpose of their own accord; rather, the majority would open their mouths to receive the proffered food but in no way lift a hand to earn it. Gratitude, especially the momentary subordination of self-interest to a higher purpose, is a characteristic which one will look for vainly in most proletarians. But the less such people do when only their virtue is appealed to, the greater the things they will carry out under the influence of some physical or moral compulsion, under the control based on certain benefits of a regulation binding the chaotic masses. The same people who if left today to their own devices, plunder, rob, and destroy, who disperse like a flock of crows before the first uniformed officer, are tomorrow under the influence of a fanaticism homologous to their intellectual perception, or, under the domination of discipline whether maintained by the guillotine or by the police corporal's club, irresistible champions of and victorious workers for the greatest causes. A "compulsion" which violates no sacred human right, in which the possibility of enslavement is not inherent, which has the semblance of free will and the final result of which shall be the maturing of a judicious free will, such a "compulsion" is the guiding light for the success of a transatlantic proletariat-colony.

But how shall one find in America, the land of the greatest personal liberty and self-dependence, such a "compulsion"? For the Americans, there is none; in fact, they require none, for they are a sensible people, knowing how to help themselves, how to make laws for themselves, and, what is even more difficult, how to respect these laws. Even for the newly transplanted proletarian there is no political nor governmental "compulsion," but rather something else which is to be found in his dependence, in his accustomed reliance on guardianship, but particularly in his deep-seated tendency to look for his livelihood from above. No man can command the proletarian, sent over at the expense of a national endeavor, or have at his disposal their labor-power according to some regulated plan for some purpose, even though this would be their proper or characteristic existence. The whole relationship of the leaders and those led depends upon a simple condition of contract, the *causa movens* of which is the breadbasket. The reciprocal relationship of the society with the emigrants lasts only for one year, and that actually only during the year before the harvest; its problem, therefore, is to utilize this short period of time in such a way that the protected as well as the protector attain their goal. Only during the first year, when the immigrant is being provisioned, can one with any likelihood expect him to respect the society's claim to his services; whatever is done voluntarily by the immigrant after this period of dependence on the breadbasket is a rare exception. Only after a period of years, perhaps first through his children, will the proletarian realize and appreciate what has been done for him; and every transatlantic administration based on the high-mindedness of those people and lacking any material foundation will soon see through tragic experience the collapse of the whole undertaking. It frequently was my sad experience, not only among many of the proletariat sent over and provisioned gratis by the Adelsverein, but also with some of the former members of our society, to discover that with spiritual proletarians the voice of reason reveals itself like the voice of the preacher in the wilderness and that the transition from irrational thinking to rational action must be brought about by means other than by mere persuasion. Some will criticize me and claim that the mere dependence on food and agricultural aid is not sufficient coercion to lead people in industry, discipline, and the performing of work organized according to plan; but, in this respect, the many experiences in Texas have proved sufficiently that a piece of bread, apparently tendered in conjunction with the alluring prospect of early independence, has the greatest effect on people of that kind. As early as on the ocean trip, it is almost unbelievable what an influence a tasty morsel, a double portion, and the like, has with the steerage passengers; much greater will be the effect of an assured piece of bread for a whole year. It really is not the work itself which discourages most of the proletariat; rather it is the trouble one must take to find work. This circumstance alone will deter most of them from breaking away from the colonization enterprise and trying to establish themselves independently of the support and leadership of the society. For them it is a terrifying thought to look for work among strangers, most of them people speaking a different language, and they prefer to be guaranteed a sure livelihood among their countrymen in exchange for a prescribed course of action. I have seen how the inhabitants of Fredericksburg under the administration of the notorious Dr. Schubart[55] put up with every possible shocking outrage at the hands of that person, with the most abject submission merely to receive the meager provisions of which he was the administrator; and I

[55] Dr. Johann Schubart apparently received complete power (*Vollmacht*) from Louis Cappes, a Society official in Texas, to control the distribution of provisions in Fredericksburg in early 1847 when those provisions were getting scarce. According to his own letter, he was forced to use stringent measures to forestall famine in Fredericksburg in the summer of 1847. *Solms-Braunfels Archiv*, XLIII, 152ff, 83ff.

believe it can be almost categorically assumed that out of every thousand of the proletariat who spend a whole year in the manner I have proposed, nine hundred will gladly submit to every regulation. To be sure, every pretense of freedom of choice has to be avoided, but in every regulation it must be kept in mind that irrational people not be allowed to remain irrational but be transformed into self-thinking people. I have seen such striking examples of the happy result of the benevolent exercise of the authority of the breadbasket on utterly barbarous people that I do not consider anything impossible anymore in this respect, especially when the administrative personnel who design the plan and a goodly number of right-thinking people become animated with the spirit of harmony, work, and the hope of an early independent future for the workers. But above all, unity in the leadership of the European directorship and confidence in the character of their Texas officers must prevail, for this will cause a corresponding trust on the part of the emigrants in their leaders. Mistrust is the death of such an undertaking, a poor official being worth more than a suspected one—for this reason one should be severe in the selection of leaders but then fully rely on their leadership. A public rendering of accounts at appointed times is here a prime requisite.

I want to discuss next the several points in detail:

a) *Transportation from the seaport to the colony.*

This is best achieved by means of durable oxen-drawn vehicles equipped with wooden axles, with which one can carry a load of 4,500 to 5,000 pounds with four yoke of oxen. The average day's journey is about twelve to eighteen English miles, because, unlike horses which graze practically the entire night if they have been worked during the day, oxen should be hitched up later in the morning and unhitched earlier in the evening than mules or horses, needing additionally several hours rest to chew their cud. Generally the transportation should take place only in the late fall, because the immigrant can then immediately begin his field work, the period of provisioning from the storehouses of the colonization society being thus only nine months (from November to August). The wagons are so arranged that there is room on them for weary women and children as well as for the supplies necessary for the nine months for the first group of immigrants and for later increments of settlers, foodstuffs such as salt and coffee which cannot be produced in the colony during the first year; there is also room for necessary implements, clothes, medicines, and the like. Since the period of their use as a means of transport lasts only a few months (from October to December), the acquired wagons and teams can be otherwise employed during the entire period of the other nine months in the hauling of lumber and fence rails, and later, after the colony has grown and produces valuable products, in the transporting of these products back to the seaport and other places.

The necessary teamsters are to be chosen from the ranks of the immigrants with the understanding that in this way they have done their share in the colonizing effort and that all economic labor necessary to their existence in the following year and labor in raising dwellings will be done for them by the other colonists. The same system can be followed in regard to blacksmith and wagon shops and can later even be extended to the manufacture of new wagons by the craftsmen among the immigrants. For the first two or three years the latter is impossible, for a sufficient number of wagons which the transportation of the yearly shipment of proletarians demands must be acquired ready-made. It would even not be inexpedient in the first few years to have special teamsters who are not members of the colony.

b) *Provisioning for the first year.*

This extremely important chapter deserves a very close analysis since the fate of the entire undertaking is dependent upon the proper handling of this problem. What a single person requires for a livelihood over a period of nine months is easy to compute; it is equally easy to calculate that this provisioning, if it is done in the manner of the military or as the Adelsverein has accorded their protégés, requires sums that exceed the means of any colonization society. A few figures may serve to illustrate this statement. An adult worker or person needs for his maintenance monthly:

Corn, 1 bushel or	50 lbs.,	cost...............	0.40
Beef,	20 lbs.,	"	0.40
Coffee,	2 lbs.,	"	0.16
Salt	¼ lbs.,	"	0.11
Bacon,	3 lbs.,	"	0.30
Total pounds	75¼	Total cost........	$1.27[56]

[56] As given in the original text. The correct sum should be $1.37.

The price is based on what these items usually cost in the more distant settlements, which will, of course, be closest to any newly established colony. But this price situation will turn out to be far more unfavorable, and, in the case of most articles, will probably double as soon as a larger number of emigrants arrive all at once. All disadvantages to which the buyer who unconditionally needs an article is subject, all disadvantages arising out of a market overcrowded with buyers and comparatively poor (at least for the moment) in goods, will then converge and give the profiteers free rein. At the same time it must be borne in mind that the provisions might possibly have to be transported a great distance from the place of purchase to the projected colony and that there is a considerable freight charge of 75¼ pounds, which, of course, because of the self-established transportation system based on the labor of the colonists is not a cash expenditure but which, because of the labor power of the draft animals and teamsters that must be expended, is to be reckoned quite highly.

For nine months that sum amounts to a total of 11 dollars and 43 cents or 28 florins and 35 kreuzers in money costs for the provisioning of one person. This amounts to $57.15 or 142 florins and 52 kreuzers per family of five. A thousand families would necessitate a money outlay for provisions of some 143,-000 florins in one year, and what are one thousand families when the question is the great scarcity of time and need for a regulated emigration to remedy the overpopulation problem. How great might this total probably get when the above mentioned hindrances of the profiteer and the temporary scarcity of the goods will perhaps double the price of the supplies? How soon would the estimate of provisioning costs be barely adequate for half of the actual amount, resulting in famine, loss of credit, disorder in the management, lack of discipline, and complete destruction of the mutual trust so greatly necessary as happened in the case of the Adelsverein to the injury of the contractors and the emigrants. Thus, another way must be found to avoid this drawback. If we consider the single items in my computed monthly estimate of food provisions, we find that, except for coffee and salt, all sustenance necessities can

---

The 10 cents error in the addition in the table is carried through into the subsequent calculations.

be produced within the country itself, and this leads to the following very simple statement and to the complete solution of the difficulties of the question of provisions. *The colonization society must itself produce the provisions necessary to the sustenance of each increment of emigrants during the first cropless year and in such a way that the human labor necessary be performed gratis by those colonists that are that year dependent on the administration.* The management in Texas has to keep the following in mind:

1) The annual dispatchings of emigrants must be in such numbers that the newcomers each year may obtain their entire food needs from the previous harvest and therefore make any expenditures unnecessary.
2) The work of the emigrants during the year they are dependent on the community larder must be so organized that they not only will be able to supply their own wants of the next year, but also the needs of the following increment for the next nine months. After a careful examination, the following main considerations will appear.

A. *Corn.* A family of five requires some eighty bushels of corn for its yearly sustenance as well as an equal amount for their work animals, chickens, hogs, and other animals—part of this as feed and part to get them accustomed to their house.

All of this is predicated on a holding of ten acres of cultivable land. One acre of land produces on an average twenty bushels of corn the first year, thirty the second year, sixty to eighty bushels the following year; on ten acres this amounts to the sum of two hundred, three hundred, six hundred, and eight hundred bushels, respectively. A family of five, however, requires for their support during the nine months of their first year forty-five bushels as provisions plus about four bushels for seed-corn, thus a total of only some 50 bushels. It follows from these facts that even from the small tract of ten acres which each colonist receives, almost the entire needs of the next year's increment can be drawn. I say almost because, in this case, only the yield of the first harvest, some 200 bushels, can be considered since the colonist is only during the first year dependent on the society; but such a management would be subject to the following drawbacks:

1) it will be difficult to find the legal means to induce the immigrant to give up corn which he has raised upon his own

land to which he has a valid title given him by the society. Mere gratitude and a regard for equity cannot, as already noted, be counted upon among the proletariat. And it might be difficult to devise a simple, just solution in every respect, apart from a tax-in-kind, which gives rise to fraud and other unpleasantries of which everyone is cognizant who has had experience with the collection of a tithe in kind here in Germany with its thousand-year-old tenure and vassalage customs.

2) every subsequent increment of emigrants would have to be smaller than the previous one, because the 200 bushels of the first harvest would not completely supply the needs of a new emigrant family after deduction of the needs of the prior one.

A family of five can live quite well on the produce of ten acres and can even achieve a certain affluence through the subsequent culture of more valuable products. Ten acres, however, are by no means the maximum which they can cultivate with their labor power. We can, without erring, count on double that amount for such a family.

Thus the plan would strongly suggest that after working the ten acres belonging to him, the emigrant should during the first year (that is, as long as one has legal claim on his services) apply his extra working hours to the cultivation of a large farm owned by the colonization society. In this way the necessary grain for the next increment of settlers would be produced by the increment of the previous year without any extra expense for the labor used. The company farm must therefore be large enough to afford sufficient sustenance for the number of families coming the following fall. Thus it appears that during the first year of the settlement for, say 1,000 new emigrant families, an area of approximately 2,500 acres of land will be needed to produce the requisite amount of 50,000 bushels of corn (because for the first year the average production is only 20 bushels per acre); during the second year the cultivation of the same acreage will produce 75,000 bushels, and during the third year 150 to 200,000 bushels. This surplus can be used to palliate the effects of partial crop failures as well as to supply the needs mentioned below.

B. *Meat.* Relatively little labor is necessary to provide meat since it is only necessary to procure in the beginning a sufficient stock of cattle whose natural yearly increase will meet the meat needs of the annual quota of emigrants. The establishment of large stock farms in suitable places and the management of these in such a way that the number of cattle butchered yearly will not be greater than the natural increase are the means by which the colony will be supplied with its meat requirements without cost after the original equipment and the foundation cattle stock have been paid for. The workers needed to care for and drive the cattle to the separate settlements can be drawn from the whole body of emigrants under the same arrangement as were the teamsters and recruited each year from the new arrivals. The accompanying detailed outline gives a survey of the costs and equipment which will provide the meat and bacon needs of the colony. Again in this case the enormous advantages for the establishment of a proletarian colony which Texas enjoys over the northern United States are set forth in the clearest light, since only in Texas is such a colossal cattle industry possible, without toil, independent of agriculture, and supplying the immigrants with meat raised by themselves. I want to mention here that I have purposely set all estimates of provision needs unusually high in order that all unforeseen situations, which whenever estimates are figured too closely react to the detriment of the participators, will be reckoned with in advance by fixing the estimate higher than necessary. This is all the more necessary considering the chances of a great famine that can arise in a very short time among a large body of people insufficiently provided with food, since it is well known it takes only four days for a person to die of hunger whereas many weeks will elapse in case of faulty budgeting before relief can be effected. I do not think that I need to justify the inclusion of coffee as one of the necessities of life. Anyone acquainted with the salutary effect of this economical drink on a backwoodsman's life to which the German is quite unaccustomed will agree with me that this staple is a necessary one.

But now the question is, how shall the provisions for the first shipment of emigrants, for instance, the first thousand families, be acquired? The answer is already partially apparent in what I have written above. Above all, the provisions must be at hand before the emigrants arrive so that the undertaking does not begin with lack of supplies and disorder as was the case with the earlier Adelsverein. The stock farms must be put into operation at such a time to make it possible that the year's meat production will be available the following fall for the number of emigrants arriving at that time. The same is true of the farm which is to furnish the necessary corn. The necessary improvements for both establishments must also be bought at least a year prior to the arrival of the actual settlers, and the workers required for these purposes must be available at the same time. Just how the work shall be undertaken, as well as several special points, is shown in the outline.

c) *Supplying the necessary field and building implements and tools.*

To engage in agriculture, a certain number of implements and work animals are indispensable, and the supplying of these to the colonists at the right time is an absolute requisite for the fulfillment of the given purpose. As a general rule, an emigrant family needs the following implements and tools to cultivate its fields, to build houses, and to build enclosures:

1. one breaking-plow, at a cost of	$ 12.00
2. two ox-chains, to be used also as log-chains (chains used to drag beams)	8.00
3. one ax	1.25
4. one shingle knife	.25
5. one carving knife	.25
6. two paring-chisels	1.00
7. one hatchet (handaxe-hammer combination)	.50
8. one grinding stone	2.00
9. one post-hole digger [57]	3.00
10. one heavy oxen-wagon	80.00
11. one pickaxe	.50
12. one hoe	.50
13. one spade	1.00
14. one cross-cut saw	3.00
15. one brush	1.00
16. files	.50
17. cooking and baking utensils	2.00
18. two yoke oxen	60.00
	$176.75

or in guilders about 430 florins.

[57] In the German printing, Herff uses the term, "Dollenbohrer" (Rollenbohrer) which is a small rotating auger, but it is apparent he has a tool for digging post-holes in mind here.

The outfitting of a thousand families thus would come to some four hundred thousand guilders, a sum which far exceeds what it would be possible to raise. Let me state, however, that I have based the prices in this estimate on the selling price of those articles in New Orleans and, in the case of the draft oxen, on the average price of such animals in Texas. It is immediately apparent that it would be possible to supply those articles from German or English factories at a price one-third lower; however, they would have to be equal to American instruments in quality and utility of shape. There is a greater difference between a Collins axe[58] and a German woodcutter's axe than there is between a Damascus sword and a regular army sword, and all instruments must be adapted to the climatic conditions, the kind of woods, the soil over there; in short, to the differences between America and Europe. This matter requires special attention; here the Adelsverein once more has shown how it should not be done; at that time all of the tools it furnished were made in European factories and were at the most but imperfect copies of American patterns or even completely new tools invented as adaptable to Texas by German speculators but which had no utility other than as scrapiron. These tools can be furnished so much cheaper because they will be free of import duties in that they can be imported as personal property, being handicraft tools, thus allaying any suspicion that they might become trading goods. In spite of this possible reduction in the total costs, the necessary sum still remains so considerable that the whole undertaking would be frustrated were it not that ways and means for the reduction of these costs can be found, as has in Texas in many cases already been proved to be practical. *This means is realized in the merger of a certain number of families into a larger group, doing the combined necessary work with relatively much fewer tools, so that the purchases which according to the outline above are necessary for the needs of one family, with adequate organization, in the case of some tools will suffice for a number of families and, in the case of others, need to be increased but relatively little.*

I want to elaborate this statement by citing an example in

[58] The Collins axe is a small, peculiarly American axe, small enough to be carried on a woodsman's belt. See "Collins ax" in *A Dictionary of American English*, I.

some detail. A colony of approximately twenty families, in order to make in nine months a first crop sufficient for themselves as well as for the provisioning of the next equally large shipment of colonists destined for the colony, has to do the following necessary work:

1) build twenty block houses;
2) break 200 acres of land and plant and cultivate corn for their own use;
3) fence in those acres;
4) plant and cultivate 50 acres of corn to furnish provisions for the second shipment of colonists;
5) build a good cattle corral of at least one-half acre size.

These jobs have a varying urgency since several of them, for instance, breaking the land, the corral, and partly also the construction of the houses, should be done right in the beginning and with the greatest possible haste, while the further cultivation of the fields, fence-building, and such are jobs of lesser urgency and can be carried out with less haste. Out of 20 families of five members each, one can take for granted without calculating too high or too low that there will be an average of twenty-five men fitted to do all jobs, plus five boys, aged eight to ten years, able to do certain tasks, such as driving oxen, leading the plow-oxen, and tending the unhitched work animals, and so forth. In any practical arrangement of work, each individual family should not have to build its own house and fences, but these tasks should be done by an adequate number of men reciprocally for all. In this way, through hard work and, what is here most important, expense-saving utilization of field and other implements, the relationship of individual jobs will be approximately the following:

1) to break the land, for which there is only three months time, November, December, and January, there will be needed, during the 65 working days, 22 per month, the following:

a) five plows with 15 yoke oxen,
b) five adult workers, to plow,
c) five boys to lead the oxen.

In this manner the 250 acres needed by the present and the next year's colonists can easily be broken within the allotted time in 65 working days without any extraordinary effort on the part of beast or man, since each team and plow operated in this manner will turn over three-fourths of an acre daily.

2) for the equally pressing task of building the block houses the following will be needed:

a) one thousand logs for twenty houses, fifty per house;

b) 400 rafters and 800 boards;

c) thatch and wattle[59] for roofing.

The logs and lumber can be felled and cut in fourteen days by ten men, who will not have to work too hard; the same [building material] hauled to its destination with two oxen-wagons, three yoke of oxen per wagon, and four drivers in eighteen days (both groups will commence work at the same time); then, after the expiration of the eighteen days, the houses can be erected and equipped with fireplaces in ten days by the same fourteen woodcutters and drivers, and finally stoutly roofed with thatch in another ten days—a total of thirty-eight working days altogether.

The tools necessary for this work are: fourteen axes, two cross-cut saws, three back-saws, two post-hole diggers, twelve hatchets, two oxen wagons, six strong chains, six yoke oxen, four paring-chisels, four files (for the saws), and four planing knives.

3) To enclose 200 acres, if the field is rectangular, 12,600 fence rails (which must be ten feet long and ⅓ foot thick) are needed; further, 3800 stakes and riders[60] are needed, a total of 16,400.

We have in mind here a large community field and not the separate enclosing of the twenty ten-acre plots which belong to the individual families; to do the latter would take no fewer than 72,800 fence rails, stakes, and riders, and consequently also a considerably greater number of working days. This is once more striking evidence of how communal management profits the partakers. There is ample time from when the houses have been finished till the end of March to complete the field enclosure, some three months with about 65 working days. However, if the same men which were used as woodcutters and drivers in the building of the houses are used here to fell trees, split, haul, and set up the rails, that is, to completely build the enclosure, only fifty working days at the most will be

---

[59] Herff uses the word *watte*, for which the best English word would be "wattle," which is a twig or withe for making a framework.

[60] A "rider" in a rail fence is the top rail, placed in a crotch of

needed, leaving a great deal of labor power to become available anew. For that work the same tools will serve that were used in building the houses. The fifty acres belonging to the colonization society which are to serve as a source of provisions for the following shipment of emigrants I have purposely not included in the enclosure, because, in accordance with the outline above, that particular corn farm must already be in operation before the present emigrants could have been sent across.

4) to cultivate 250 acres of corn, it will be necessary to have:
   a) the same number of plows with fifteen yoke oxen and ten tillers and team drivers;
   b) five spades, five hoes, and five grubbing hoes to work certain spots infested with scrub brush or weeds and to work a garden plot.

Besides the necessary implements and teams, in order to thoroughly cultivate the field the men will need to put in the following number of working days:
   a) Harrowing the field (with home-made wooden, three-cornered harrows), if five harrows are used, eight days.
   b) Drawing the seed furrows, sowing, and covering the seed, eight days.
   c) First plowing of the corn, fourteen days.
   d) Second plowing, fourteen days.
   e) Planting beans, pumpkins, and the like between the corn, four days.

This is a total of forty-eight days.

This is to be done during the period from the beginning of February to the middle of March, thus an average of fifteen to sixteen working days per month.

5) The construction of a cattle corral is a matter of only two days' work (for ten good woodcutters) and can be undertaken concurrently by the house builders without appreciably extending the labor time allotted to building the houses.

If we now compare the costs of a settlement established and maintained under this system with what they would be under the maintenance of individual families, we arrive at the following:

---

crossed stakes at the end of each panel. See "Rider" in *A Dictionary of American English*, IV.

The Regulated Emigration of the German

	Dollars	Cents
Twenty families here[61] need five plows,	60.00	
two wagons,	160.00	
twenty ox-chains,	160.00	
fourteen axes,	17.40	
two cross-cut saws,	6.00	
three back-saws,	3.00	
two post-hole diggers,	6.00	
four paring chisels,	2.00	
four files,	1.00	
four planing knives,	1.00	
twenty-one yoke oxen,	630.00	
five spades,	5.00	
five hoes,	2.50	
five grubbing hoes,	2.50	
ten shingle knives,	2.50	
one grindstone,	2.00	
cooking utensils,	10.00	
	1076.90,	
or 2692 florins.		[*sic*]

Per family of five this would amount to about 135 florins.

But even this sum will decrease because in the second year of the settlement it will not be necessary to construct houses and fences in so limited a time nor will a large amount of labor power be necessary to do the difficult job of landbreaking in so short a time.

The requirements of work animals, wagons, and plows will be reduced at least to half of what they were in the first year, being only:

three plows,	36.00	dollars
one wagon,	80.00	"
ten ox-chains,	80.00	"
eleven yoke oxen,	330.00	"

Thus, assuming the other items for building purposes as remaining the same, it is seen that the actual costs for tools and implements for twenty families will come to 592.90 dollars, that is, about 1482 florins. For each family of five, therefore, the outfitting costs to carry on farming activities come to some

---

[61] That is, under the system of cooperative utilization of implements and labor power developed in the paragraphs just preceding.

75 guilders, a sum which actually should be considerably smaller if the iron tools are manufactured in German or English factories, as mentioned above. The wagons, plows, chains, and other items which have become surplus during the second year as far as the first increment is concerned will fall to the following increment. Besides that, within a few years the full required number of work animals will not have to be bought anymore, because the stockfarm that supplies the beef cattle requirements can gradually also produce the draft animals without any further costs other than the original costs of establishing the stockfarm. I say gradually because it will take time to break in bulls and because new untrained teams can only gradually be used first as wheel oxen and then as lead and pole oxen, and finally for plowing. Likewise, at a later time a large part of the implements must be made and wagon repair work done by the craftsmen among the emigrants under the same terms as the other tasks done by the emigrants during the first year, that is, without any pay other than their allotted fields, food, and other support. By this procedure the sum of the cash expenses will once more be appreciably reduced. *One cannot draw up a definite budget of equal size for each year for a colony founded on principles such as these;* rather, the needs for the first year when everything has to be set up will require a total expenditure at least ten times greater than in the second year; in the third year again less than in the second year, and finally practically nothing. The sums spent in the first years with the dividends from them must completely cover all expenditures in the following years for provisions, tools, and transport, making new additions to capital funds unnecessary provided the colony maintains not only itself but also the annual increase. Though there are substantial savings in costs through the workplan outlined above, even greater economies are effected in the actual work itself. This work, as we know, is done without cost to the colonization society during the first year and permits it to carry out a great many undertakings without expenditures for wages by making use of the surplus labor power. The laying out of roads, workshops of different kinds, contracts which the society makes with wealthier settlers for house construction, tillage, and the like, in short, all possible undertakings for which labor is needed, can be managed in this way to the considerable advantage of all. For

Months	Work needing to be done each month toward the maintenance of the colony	Number of workers necessary		Number of days each is to work	
		Adults	Boys	Adults	Boys
Nov.	Building houses, cattle corrals	14	—	22	—
	Breaking the land	5	5	22	22
Dec.	Building houses, cattle corrals	14	—	16	—
	Land breaking	5	5	22	22
	Splitting fence rails	14	—	6	—
Jan.	Land breaking	5	5	22	22
	Splitting fence rails	14	—	22	—
Feb.	Harrowing & planting	5	5	16	16
	Splitting fence rails	14	—	22	—
March	First plowing	5	5	14	14
April	Second plowing	5	5	14	14
May	Planting beans and melons between the corn	5	5	4	4
June	—	—	—	—	—
July	—	—	—	—	—

Total number of work-days used		Total number of	
Adults	Boys	Adults	
1,782	580	4,050	

example, I again return to my twenty families. I am assuming twenty-five individuals among them fitted to do all types of work and reckon twenty-two working days for the months November to April inclusive and only ten working days for the months of May to July inclusive, the latter because of the heat, which permits work only in the morning and late afternoon. The total sum necessary for the existence of the colony and for the provisioning of the following year's shipment is given above. If we now compare the labor power and days necessary for those purposes with the total of twenty-five available workers and the working days over the given nine-months period (at 22 and 10 days), which together come to 162, the total result is a considerable surplus of time and labor-power, which the table clearly presents. [Tables above.]

This shows a surplus of labor power, which even if one as-

Proletariat with Special Reference to Texas

Total days of work for each month		Number of work-days in each month	Number of workers available in the colony		Total number of work-days possible per month		There remain at the disposal of the colonization society			
							Week-days		Work-days	
Adults	Boys		Adults	Boys	Adults	Boys	Adults	Boys	Adults	Boys
418	110	22	25	5	550	110	132	–	6	–
418	110	22	–	–	550	110	132	–	6	–
418	110	22	–	–	550	110	132	–	6	–
388	110[62]	22	–	–	550	110	162	30	6	–
60[63]	60	22	–	–	550	110	490	50	20	–
60	60	22	–	–	550	110	490	50	20	–
20	20	10	–	–	250	50	230	30	20	–
–	–	10	–	–	250	50	250	50	25	5
–	–	10	–	–	250	50	250	50	25	5

workdays available			Total number of work-days remaining at the disposal of the colonization society	
	Boys		Adults	Boys
	810		2,268	230

sumes only one half of this (1,134 adult working days and 115 youth working days) to be actually available is still big enough to offer substantial advantages to the colonization society. Anyone acquainted with the value of labor in America, who knows that with such an immense, often unused wealth in raw products and means of production it is labor only, in most cases, which one pays for, will be able to appreciate the advantage of such a large body of labor power available for use over a period of nine months. The ratio of raw materials to labor is nowhere more striking than in America. A wagonload of wood, which I cut and haul myself, costs me absolutely nothing in Texas,

---

[62] This figure should be 80 (5 x 16) rather than 110.
[63] Five times fourteen is 70, rather than 60, for both March and April. These slight inaccuracies throw off the totals at the bottom of the chart by the same amount.

The Regulated Emigration of the German

whereas a load of wood which somebody else has cut and hauled would probably cost no less than here in Germany, even though the wood itself, as I have said, can be gotten by anybody for nothing in the public forests. Likewise, anyone may make hay where he wishes, except, of course, on enclosed land, and yet a wagonload of hay, which you have had mowed and hauled for you, will cost five dollars, or about one-half guilder per hundred pounds. How much can a society that is able to command thousands of days work annually accomplish with this labor capital in industrial and trade pursuits, in road building, and the like? What a wealth of real gain would result from that; consequently what a steadily greater and more beneficent efficacy in the realization of the primary national purpose, which is at the same time philanthropic and very necessary, will be achieved from year to year!

I anticipate two principal objections by others and hence I want to take each one up separately.

1) It is impossible in practice to carry out such an organized work plan. This criticism is most conclusively refuted by citing an actual example of colonization carried out under such a system. There are many such examples, only in many of them a force other than just granting or denying nutritional and agricultural aid made its influence felt upon those engaged in carrying out the plan. It has principally been religious enthusiasm which has helped to carry out such undertakings, and very often with a great deal of luck if the opulence of the community may be called that. The establishment of the Rappists in Harmony and Economy,[64] the settlement of the Arnsburg Separatists,[65] and both the colonies of the Mormons and Shak-

---

[64] In 1804, George Rapp left Germany with about 600 adherents and founded the community of "Harmony," in Lycoming County, Pennsylvania. In 1814, they moved to Indiana, but in 1824 they sold their holdings to Robert Owen and moved back to Pennsylvania, where the settlement of Economy was founded within a few miles of Pittsburgh. After Robert Owen bought the Rappist holdings in Indiana, "Harmony" became the famed "New Harmony." Morris Hillquit, *History of Socialism in the United States* (New York and London, 1903), 32–34, 61.

[65] Undoubtedly a misprint, and probably refers to the religious sect called "The True Inspiration Society," which was formed in Armenburg, Germany, between 1820 and 1840. Christian Metz, the leader, led the congregation to America where they formed the community of Eben-Ezer, near Buffalo, New York, in 1842. In

ers⁶⁶ come under this category. I am acquainted through personal observation with several of these settlements and have even seen one of them, a Mormon settlement on the Pedernales,⁶⁷ established. For two years I have closely observed the remarkably fast growth of this undertaking begun with practically no working capital, especially noting that all community work was performed with remarkable harmony and industry by everybody. I want, however, to steer away completely from such establishments springing from fanaticism, since that motive is lacking in the case at hand. I am equally as reluctant to talk of our own society, built upon a similar working arrangement that developed beyond all expectations, inasmuch as only cultured persons, who, because they understand each other more readily and are more rational collaborators, participated. On the other hand, I can cite the settlement of Leiningen and Castell⁶⁸ as a perfectly fitting example. *Founded by Spiess,*

1855, they moved to Iowa, where the well-known utopian community of Amana was established. Hillquit, *History of Socialism in the United States*, 37–40.

⁶⁶ The Society of the Shakers is one of the oldest sectarian societies in the United States, the first Shaker settlement having been established in New York in 1776. They are primarily a religious sect, and the violent contortions of their bodies when they receive revelation from the spirit world earned them the name of "Shakers." Communism is part of their well-ordered and healthful mode of life, but it extends to the family only, there being no community property. Some families may be quite large, however. The sect reached its zenith in the second quarter of the nineteenth century. Hillquit, *History of Socialism in the United States*, 29–31.

⁶⁷ This Mormon colony of some 200 men, women, and children was established in 1847 on the Pedernales some four miles south of Fredericksburg, and seems to have gotten along quite well with the Germans, although there was some political friction. They built a mill to grind corn which the Society officials utilized, since it apparently was the only mill in the general area. The colony left in 1853. *Solms-Braunfels Archiv*, XLIII, 149; XLIV, 80; LII, 69. See also Don Biggers, *German Pioneers in Texas* (Fredericksburg, 1925), 94–96.

⁶⁸ Castell and Leningen were founded soon after the Bettina company settled on the Llano. Although Herff claims that Castell was founded by Hermann Spiess, it was laid out before Spiess became commissioner-general, and credit should go to Meusebach. Although the settlers started out with such a work plan as Herff here outlines, Biesele states that the plan of community cooking and housekeeping was abandoned soon after they arrived on the Llano. Both settlements were located on the north bank of the

these originally destitute, now well-established settlements on the Llano sent over by the Adelsverein, which are made up in large part of very uncultured and partly of rather ill-famed persons, have, with a much smaller supporting capital and because of the poor credit rating of the Mainzer Verein, under very unfavorable conditions in the matter of provisions, cultivated their fields with few animals and very few implements, built their houses following such a work plan, and have in this way with relatively insignificant cost assured their existence.[69]
While the earlier settlements of the Verein, founded without such a plan, raised barely enough food during the second year for their needs, those cited even made a surplus crop in the first year. It can be maintained with certainty that had that system been followed earlier at the time of the founding of the Verein colonies, half of the sum which that undertaking cost would have been saved. I admit it would have been difficult for anyone other than Spiess to inaugurate anything of that sort; whereas he, contemporaneously with the Verein's colony that labored under the dictatorship of bread need, had another colony nearby, which likewise worked collectively, whose deep-rooted motive was not the need of eating and drinking but rather the realization that only in this way could something great be accomplished with small means and to labor with all one's might for the highly promising German colony. The proximity of our company to those settlements not only proved to be an example to them of how it was possible with meager means but with united and efficiently organized strength to accomplish something big, but also by word and deed has beneficently affected the spiritual life of those settlements made up of heterogenous and barbaric elements. When quarrels had to be settled, neighborly aid to be given, or any worthwhile improvement to be made, we feared neither the labor nor the eruptions of barbarism quite often directed against us in the beginning. Instead we always sought to awaken the spirit of

---

Llano, within a few miles of Bettina, Castell above and Leningen below that settlement. Castell is the only one of these settlements which survived, and, oddly enough, is today on the south bank of the Llano. Biesele, *The History of the German Settlements in Texas, 1831–1861*, pp. 152–154.

[69] Hermann Spiess, co-founder with Herff of the Bettina colony, became director-general of the Society in July, 1847.

order, of peace, and of industry there where earlier largely only strife and idleness had reigned. We soon saw the fruits of our endeavors; we saw how a small number of resolute, intelligent, and honest men, working together, present an infinitely greater moral and even physical power than the chaotic mob. When the Indians appeared to menace our settlements that lay beyond the military border, the majority sought aid with the minority, and our homes became for several nights the sanctuary for our six-times more numerous neighbors. Only our persuasion and support succeeded in keeping the colonists, so boastful before but so despairing during the danger, from moving back to the lower settlements behind the military frontier, and thus we induced the government, which thereby was furnished with proof of the steadfastness of the colonies, to extend the protecting military cordon to the Llano after some months. The recent deliberations on this matter in the Legislature in Austin, and the letters of the Governor of Texas to Spiess[70] concerning those affairs, furnish evidence that our firmness at that time was recognized in places other than in the Ranger camps or the blockhouses of Castell and Leiningen. The one year which we spent on the Llano has proved to me again how easy it is to awaken the spirit of order and industry even among the most intractable and barbaric people if along with kindly instruction another cultural influence is exerted.

2) The second objection concerns itself with the future lot of the settlers who were obliged during the first year to engage in communal labor because of the influence of the breadbasket. What will happen, it is asked, when that dictatorship ends? Is it after all a good fortune, worthy of being called an existence, to spend one's life under such fettering bonds with the restraint on individuality through the absorption of the individual in the whole? All of the numerous criticisms usually levied against the different socialistic systems will here again be heard, and Icaria, Phalanstére, Fourier, and Cabet[71] will be the rallying

[70] These letters are not in the *Solms-Braunfels Archiv*. Spiess apparently did not preserve them.

[71] Etienne Cabet, French communist and social reformer, published in 1848 his famous book, *Voyage to Icaria*, in which he described a utopia in which the government alone engaged in commerce and supervised work and education. Some followers did sail for Texas in 1848 to establish an Icarian city, and the next year Cabet himself came to Illinois to establish such a city in Illinois

cry of all those who damn with words rather than with argument. Indeed, this has already partially happened in advance, in that an ill-advised and malevolent correspondent of the *Darmstädter Zeitung* has already more than once portrayed me as the preacher of a new Utopia, our society as a kind of partner to Cabet, and Texas as the happy Eldorado of the dreamers and visionaries. Although the reader may already have had the chance to pass judgment as to whether anyone has the right to make this accusation, I deem it to be necessary, considering the great fear which many a sincere gaffer undergoes at the mere mention of the words communist, Cabet, Phalanstére, and Icaria, here once more openly and directly to protest against our, or my, participation in such foolish institutions as Icaria and Phalanstére or such equally foolish personalities as Cabet and Fourier. Texas and Iowa or any other state of the Union can never be an Eldorado, an Icaria, for a man who has seen those lands and has become acquainted with their resources as well as the hard work connected with a colonization enterprise. It is not my aim to prove any system, idea, or any other theory practical by the establishment of colonies organized on the above principles, but rather the purpose is merely to make the largest number of proletarians self-supporting in the shortest possible time and with the lowest possible expenditure. If anyone can offer a means other than the one I have suggested for the fulfillment of this purpose, I will gladly put aside my opinion, not because I consider it unfeasible, but because the personnel forces, which have to accomplish such a thankless task as is the organization of ignorant and undisciplined masses,

---

upon a communistic principle. The colony prospered at first, but eventually ended in failure. Andre Lichtenberger, in *Encyclopaedia of the Social Sciences* III, 131–132. See also Albert Shaw, *Icaria, A Chapter in the History of Communism* (New York and London, 1884), which gives the complete story of the Icarians, including their Texas venture.

Francois Marie Charles Fourier was one of the most famous of the utopian socialist writers of the early nineteenth century. He worked out a plan of a harmonious society in great detail, the fundamental unit of which was the phalanx (phalanstére). A phalanx is composed of 1,620 persons cultivating 5,000 acres of land, each individual following his impulses or passions and in so doing acting not only in his own interest, but in the interest of the community or society as a whole. Edward S. Mason, in *Encyclopaedia of the Social Sciences* VI, 402–404.

could then carry out an easier and more pleasant undertaking. The problem of the colonizing society is not in any sense the continuing supervision of the fate of its emigrants, but rather to provide only for the means of existence and the actual manpower during the first year; that is, provide for a piece of productive land and the making of the first crop. Once this purpose is fulfilled, it is up to the immigrants, who during the first year have become acquainted with all the advantages and disadvantages of communal management and who are protected against need for another year, in what respect they want to continue or not to continue the previous year's operations. Stark necessity will force them to adopt the old plan with large or small modifications during the first two or three years since only in this way will the few implements and the small number of work animals be of help to the individual. Gradually, however, this situation will change. Wealthy settlers will seek out a place where cheap day labor can be had, merchants will be attracted by the valuable products produced by the population there, industrial establishments will spring up and give the settlers opportunity to follow other pursuits than just agriculture. Independent craftsmen will soon find it more lucrative to sell their small field plot and find their livelihood in town. By their industry many colonists soon will be in a position to own their own herds, implements, and work animals and to acquire more lands by purchase; some will look for easier and more remunerative work as factory workers, and the earlier suppression of individual enterprise, caused by the force of circumstances, will soon give way to the greatest and freest development of independence. Perhaps, though, many useful things, many a worthwhile idea, many a good arrangement of the first year's cooperative system of the colony will remain and be further developed in some distinctive manner. Unity, order, and industry, at least, will not easily disappear and that will make it an easy matter for education, which through schools will soon become general, to penetrate the minds of the masses. And in all these proceedings, the colonization society is the leader, it is the nerve of the life of the colony, it is the red thread which runs through the whole. It will have to awaken worthy endeavors, it will have to start industrial establishments and cultural and educational institutions, but it will itself also enjoy the advantages of trade and industry and through opportune utilization of them acquire more and more means with which even greater numbers of people can be sent over. Truly, it is an undertaking that if realized will more than repay the money sacrifice involved and that is worthy of the highminded and able efforts which its consummation calls forth.

d) *Leadership of the emigrants sent across.*

The biggest part of this question has already been answered in the foregoing chapter. It will suffice here once more to call attention to the fact that confidence is the basis of the undertaking, as much in regard to the relation of the transatlantic business managers to the European directors as to the relations of the former to the emigrants; the selection of the personnel who direct and execute the venture remains the chief concern. Complete knowledge of the practical aspects of colonization, familiarity with farming and cattle-raising conditions, especially personal experience therein, are indispensable. To this, however, must be added a complete knowledge of the American mercantile and industrial as well as the applicable legal situation, which might come up for discussion in the undertaking under consideration, e.g., land acquisition contracts and the like. Humanity, but also vigorous energy with only one purpose in mind, must go hand in hand with a knowledge of the inclinations and faults of the poor. To answer these purposes it is evidently necessary, where possible, to entrust that kind of a position to persons who have already been in America for some time and know intimately the considerable differences between conditions over there and in this country. It would be a big mistake to let the officials learn by experience for several years, the cost of which the colonization society and the emigrant would finally have to bear. This is valid to an almost greater degree in regard to the experts to be appointed to a preliminary research commission. It takes the European, particularly the German, at least half a year beyond the ocean to discover the standard by which one must measure North American conditions. He who goes over as a purely private individual, who pursues only his own purposes, will in that half year as a greenhorn come to only a few wrong conclusions and commit but few rash actions. It is quite a different matter with respect to an agent of a European colonization society. The speculations of the landholders, the interest of the several states in the advantages to be gained from immigration, in short, all elements which have something to gain or lose from such a grandiose undertaking as a national colonization scheme, will rush in on the research committee and present their own selfish advantages in a false light; woe to the committee, woe to the national society, but doubly woe to the emigrants, if inexperienced Europeans are subjected to such doings. America, particularly Texas, contains a goodly number of intelligent, honest, and well-intentioned Germans who have acquired experience and are willing enough to place all their strength and talents at the disposal of a national undertaking which must become historically world important. In Missouri, in Illinois, in Wisconsin live hundreds of educated and honest men, some of whom were already laudably or honorably known in the old country. In Texas, a great amount of preliminary work for colonization has already been done. Colonization is already in the sinews and blood of the Germans over there, and questions, which are riddles to the uninformed European, can be answered by every boy over there. The societies in New York or New Orleans are not the ones who can solve the actual practical problems of a grandiose colonization scheme. Like the whole existence of the members, their function is confined to the scope of the city limits.

Their advice can be of benefit only in regard to mercantile conditions, questions of transport, and in regard to crafts and professions.

In the backwoods and on the rolling prairies are to be found those really able to answer questions on colonization, for here are the men who, in addition to a European education, can call upon the experiences of a practical and active frontier life. He who has himself swung an ax, who has raised the wheat for his own bread, who has suffered the hardships of backwoods life and yet preserved for himself the advantages of education which enable one to draw separate facts into a composite whole, he alone knows the great problem, he alone will be able to work it out successfully. It will be easy, especially in Texas where, as heretofore mentioned, a school of colonization, so to speak, has been founded on a large scale, to interest the greater part of the Germans resident there in a national colony.

The participation of the higher-class and more able persons will in every case exceedingly benefit such a cause and be to it such a support as cannot be bought with money.

BIBLIOGRAPHY

Primary Sources

Bracht, Viktor. *Texas in Jahre 1848.* Elberfeld und Iserlohn: J. Baedeker, 1849.
MacDonald, William, ed. *Selected Documents Illustrative of the History of the United States, 1776–1861.* New York: The Macmillan Company, 1909.
Minot, George, ed. *The Statutes at Large and Treaties of the United States of America from December 1, 1845, to March 31, 1851, Arranged in Chronological Order, with References to the Matters of Each Act and to the Subsequent Acts on the Same Subject.* Boston: Little, Brown and Company, 1857.
Sayles, John, ed. *The Constitutions of the State of Texas, with the Reconstruction Acts of Congress, the Constitution of the Confederate States and of the United States.* Annotated. St. Louis: The Gilbert Book Company, 1884.
Solms-Braunfels Archiv. 70 Typescript Volumes. The University of Texas Archives.

Secondary Sources

Biesele, Rudolph L. *The History of the German Settlements in Texas, 1831–1861.* Austin, Texas: Privately published by Author, 1930.
Bigelow, Poultney. *History of the German Struggle for Liberty.* 4 Volumes. New York and London: Harper and Brothers, 1905.
Biggers, Don H. *German Pioneers in Texas. A Brief History of Their Hardships, Struggles and Achievements.* Gillespie County Edition. Fredericksburg, Texas: Fredericksburg Publishing Company, 1925.
Craigie, Sir William A. and Hulbert, James R., eds. *A Dictionary of American English. On Historical Principles.* 4 Volumes. Chicago: University of Chicago Press, 1938.
Der Grosse Brockhaus. Handbuch des Wissens in zwanzig Baenden. Leipzig, Germany: F. A. Brockhaus, 1928.

Dwight, Mary Ann. *Grecian and Roman Mythology.* New York: A. S. Barnes and Company, 1855.

Encyclopaedia Brittanica. 24 Volumes. Chicago, London, Toronto: Encyclopaedia Brittanica, Incorporated, 1948.

Encyclopaedia of the Social Sciences. 24 Volumes. New York: The Macmillan Company, 1947.

Henderson, Ernest F. *A Short History of Germany.* 2 Volumes. New York: The Macmillan Company, 1916.

Herff, Ferdinand Peter. *The Doctors Herff: A Three-Generation Memoir.* 2 Volumes. San Antonio, Texas: Trinity University Press, 1973.

Hillquit, Morris. *History of Socialism in the United States.* New York and London: Funk and Wagnalls, 1903.

Nixon, Pat Ireland. *A Century of Medicine in San Antonio. The Story of Medicine in Bexar County, Texas.* San Antonio, Texas: Privately Published by the Author, 1936.

Nomad, Max. *Apostles of Revolution.* Boston: Little, Brown and Company, 1939.

Ray, Bright. *Legends of the Red River Valley.* San Antonio, Texas: The Naylor Company, 1941.

Shaw, Albert. *Icaria, a Chapter in the History of Communism.* New York and London: G. P. Putnam's Sons, 1884.

Tiling, Moritz. *History of the German Element in Texas from 1820–1850 and Historical Sketches of the German Texas Singers' League and Houston Turnverein from 1853–1913.* Houston, Texas: n.p., 1913.

Tyler, Alice Felt. *Freedom's Ferment. Phases of American Social History to 1860.* Minneapolis: The University of Minnesota Press, 1944.

Veit, Valentin. *The German People. Their History and Civilization from the Holy Roman Empire to the Third Reich.* New York: Alfred A. Knopf, 1946.

Weber, Adolf Paul. *Deutsche Pioniere. Zur Geschichte des Deutschtums in Texas.* San Antonio, Texas: n.p., 1894.

Yoakum, H. *History of Texas from Its First Settlement in 1685 to Its Annexation to the United States in 1846.* 2 Volumes. Facsimile Reproduction. Austin, Texas: The Steck Company, 1935.

INDEX

Adelsverein. See Society for the Protection of German Immigrants in Texas
Albert, Duke of Coburg, xiii–xiv
Alva, Duke of, xiii
Amana, Iowa, 60–61 n. 65
Anglo-American, methods of frontier settlements, 27
Antislavery Society in America, 8
Bacon, cost of, 46
Baumgarten, Dr., 30
Behr, Ottomar von, 24
Beef: cost of, 46; planned production of, 49–51; advantages of Texas in production of, 50
Berlin, University of, xiv
Bettina, colony of: settlement of, xiv-xvi, xviii, xix, xxiv n.29.; Darmstädter company's agreement with Society for the Protection of German Immigrants in Texas, xvi–xvii; relations with Indians, xviii; abandoned, colonists return to Darmstädter Farm, xviii; considered a success by von Herff, xxi–xxii; to be first settlement in Fisher-Miller grant by Society, xxiii n.8.; location of, xxiv n.27.; mention by von Herff of, 21 n.; reference to by von Herff, 62–63
Bettina von Arnim (friend of Goethe), xxiii n. 7
Bene, Louis, xxiv n. 27, 31, 35 n
Bible Society, 8
Biesele, Rudolf L., xx, xxiii n.9
Bonn, University of, xiii
Brazos River, 18, 24
Brownsville, Texas, 37
Cabet, Etienne, 63, 64, 63–64 n.71

Cappes, Louis, 44 n
Carl, Prince of Solms-Braunfels, xvi, 31 n
Carlshafen, Texas. *See* Indianola, Texas
Castell, Count Carl von, xv, xvi, xxiv n.27
Castell, Texas, xviii, xxiv, xxiv n.27, 41, 61
Castroville, Texas, 15
Chihuahua, Mexico trade, 37–38, 41
Coffee, Colonel Holland, 28 n. 36
Coffee: cost of, 46; as a necessity of life on the frontier, 50
Coffee's Trading Post, 28 n. 36
Collins axe, 52
Colorado River (Texas), xx, 14, 24, 32
Comal River, 38
Comanche Indians, xviii, 31 n
Communal association of colonists: considered by von Herff, xvi; for groups of twenty families, 52–60; community field and cattle corral, 54–55; needs of 20 families listed, 56; economies in actual work, 57; available workers and workdays listed, 58–59; principal objections to, 60–65
Corn: basic necessity, 18–19; cost of, 46; requirements for family of five, 48; planned production of, 48–49, 53; amount needed for twenty families, 53, 55
Corpus Christi, Texas, 37
Corral, cattle, 53, 55
Cotton, 23
Darmstadt, Germany, xiii, xv–xvi
Darmstadt, Industrial School of, xvi

Index

Darmstädter Farm, xviii
Darmstädter group, xv–xviii, xxiii n.10.
Darmstädter Zeitung, 64
Der deutsche Auswanderer, xvii, 38
Die Vierziger. See Darmstädter group
Dresel, Gustav, xvii, 13 n.17, 31, 35 n
Eben-Ezer, New York, 60 n.65
Emigration, regulated, of German proletariat to Texas
  BACKGROUND AND GENERAL: summary by translator of von Herff's plan as developed in his book, xix–xxii; need for, 4; chief problems of, 6–7; importance of money in, 7–8; responsibilities of German central and community governments, 8; use of German fleet in, 8–9; advantages to German communities, 10–11; destination of, 12; consideration of other American states, 12–13
  TEXAS AS DESTINATION: wholesomeness of Texas climate, 12–13; Texas contrasted to Wisconsin, 13–15; Texas compared with Germany with respect to health, 15–16; cheapness of land and basic necessities of life, 16–22; low labor costs and less work required in Texas, 19, 20–21; advantages of producing products other than usual field crops, 22–24; successful German settlements already established, 25–26; large number of scholarly, able and prominent Germans already in Texas, 31
  COLONIZATION: acquisition of the land, 32–38; Fisher-Miller grant to be considered, 34; families to receive ten acres, provisions and tools, 38–39; use of land, 39; management of land to retain waterpower, mill and forested sites by colonizing society, 39–41; colonizing society's responsibilities, obligations and claims, 41–42, 65; transportation from the seaport to the colony, 45; provisions for the first year, 46–51; producing food needs for next group of colonists, 48; planned production of corn and meat, 48–51; needs of immigrant family listed, 51; organization of communal group by merger of twenty families, and first year needs, 52–53, communal work plan developed for, 52–60; principal objections to communal arrangement, 60–65; von Herff warns of inexperience and other problems, 65–67; value of experience of immigrants already settled in Texas, 67
Ernst, Friedrich, 15 n.21
Fences, rail, 54–55
Fisher-Miller Grant, xxiii n.8. *See also* Emigration, regulated, of German proletariat to Texas: Colonization
Florins. See Guilders
Fordtran, Charles, 15 n.21
Fourier, Francois Marie Charles, 64 n
Frankfurt, Germany, xiii
Frankfurt Parliament, 3–4, 9 n
Fredericksburg, Texas: founding of, xv, xviii, xviii n. 8; healthy settlers of, 15; family holdings in, 20; famine forestalled in, 44 n; Mormon colony near, 60–61
Gagern, Baron Heinrich von, Sr., 3
Galveston, Texas, xvi–xviii
German fleet, xx, 8–9
German government(s): lackadaisical attitude of, toward reforms in 1840s, xiv; assistance needed in colonizing effort, xx, 8–10; and questions of emigration, 3–4, 8; and Silesian famine, 15 n

72

Index

German Parliament: *See* Frankfurt Parliament
German immigrants in Texas: first settlement of, 15 n; deaths at Indianpoint, 14 n
Germany: experiences social, economic and political unrest, xiv; increased emigration to America, xiv; overpopulation of, xxii; conditions compared with English and American, 8; revolutions of 1848 in, 9 n
Giessen, Gymnasium of, xiii
Giessen, University of, xiv, xvi, xxiii n.10
Guadalupe River, 24, 32
Guilders, xvii, 7, 11, 47, 51, 56
Güttick, Belgium, xiii
Hamburg, Germany, xvii, xxiii n.10
Harmony, Indiana, 60
Hays, Colonel [Jack], 37
Heidelberg, University of, xvi
Herff, Ferdinand von
  PERSONAL LIFE: birth, xiii; education, xiii–iv; interest in botany, xiv; first man in world to open lung abcess successfully, xiv; affected by socialist ferment in Germany, xiv; co-leader of Darmstädter (Bettina) colony, xv, 13 n; visits Count Castell, xv–xvi; pledges medical attention for colony, xvii; leaves with Hermann Spiess in advance of Darmstädter group, xvii, xxiii n.10, 13 n; detains ship's captain, xviii, xxiv n.23; completes successful eye operation on Indian, xviii; describes Indians, xviii; returns to Germany and marries, xix; final emigration to America, xix; in New Braunfels, xix; in San Antonio, xix; writes manuscript of *Die Geregelte Auswanderung des deutschen Proletariats mit besonderer Beziehung auf Texas*, xix; extols virtues of Texas before Committee of the Society, xix; receives Jubilee degree from University of Giessen, xxii n.2
  THE AUTHOR: suggests planned establishments of colonies for emigrants, 6–7; on the nature of the proletariat, 10–11, 42–45, 48–49; on the advantage of Texas as site for colonization, 12–35 *passim*; is opposed to slavery, 12 n; on maintenance of German nationality in Texas, 31; begins sketch for a proletariat colony in Texas, 32; on the use and limitations of "compulsion," 43; disavows faith in socialist ideas and personalities, 63–64
Herff, Ferdinand Peter (grandson of Ferdinand von Herff, and author of *The Doctors Herff: a Three Generation Memoir*), xiii–xiv; xxii–xxiii n
Herff, Mathilde Klingelhöfer (wife of Ferdinand von Herff), xix
Hermann's University, 30–31 n.43
Houses, block, 53–54
Humboldt, Alexander von, xiii
Icaria, 30, 63–64
Illinois, 14, 22, 25, 67
Immigrants in United States, German: destitute conditions of, 4–5; antipathy toward, 5; laws regulating immigrant ships, 5; opposed to slavery, 12 n
Indianola, Texas, xviii, 14 n, 15, 25
Indianpoint, Texas. *See* Indianola, Texas
Indians: and Bettina colony, xviii; description of, by von Herff, xviii; colonization patterns in Texas affected by, 26–28; treaty with, 31 n
Industry, Texas, 15 n. 21
Iowa, xv, 8, 12–14, 18–19
Kappelhoff (ship's carpenter), xviii

Index

Know-Nothing Party. *See* Native American Party
Kreuzers, 7, 24, 47
Kriewicz, Emil, xviii
Kunzel, Dr. Heinrich, 38 n. 52
Land: methods of attainment of, xx–xxi; cheapness of, in Texas, 16–20; price of, 16–26; "league and labor," grant of, 33
Lavaca, Texas, 37
Leiningen, Texas, 31, 61
Lindheimer, Dr. Ferdinand Jacob, 30 n
Liverpool, England, xvii
Llano River, xiv, xviii–xix, xxiii n. 8, xxiv n. 27, 28, 61, 63
Mainzer Verein. *See* Society for the Protection of German Immigrants in Texas
Medina River, 32, 38
Meriwether, W. H., 37
Merryweather, Mr. *See* Meriwether, W. H.
Metz, Christian, 60 n. 65
Meusebach, John O. von, xvi, 31, 61 n. 68
Mexico, trade with, xxi, 41
Mill Creek, 15, 20, 23. *See also* Industry, Texas
Mississippi River, 14
Missouri River, 14
Mormon colony in Texas, 60–61
Nassau Farm, xvii, 35 n
National Society for German Emigration and Colonization, xv–xvi, 38 n
Native American Party, 5
New Braunfels, Texas: founding of, xv–xvi, xxiii n. 8, 28, 31; alternate site for Bettina colony, xvii; Bettina colonists return to, xix; healthy and happy settlers in, 15; land development in, 17–20, 40; natural waterpower in, 37–38
New Harmony, Indiana, 60 n. 64
New Orleans, xxiii n. 10, 4–5, 25, 37, 52
New York City, xvii, 4–5, 16
Nueces River, 28
Ohio (State), 22
Ohio River, 14
Owen, Robert, 60 n. 64
Oxen as work animals, 45–46, 51–54, 57
Pedernales River, 32, 61 n. 67
Pedernales, Texas. *See* Fredericksburg, Texas
Phalanx described, 64 n
Proletariat, German: increase in number after 1841, xiv; lack of official national concern for, 4; destitute, in New York and New Orleans, 4–5; empathetic critical appraisal of, by von Herff, 10–11; lack of gratitude of, 42–43; dependency on the breadbasket, 43–45
Rail fences: *See* Fences, rail
Rapp, George, 60 n. 64
Rappists, 60
Reaumer scale, 15
Red River Tradinghouse, 28
Riders, rail fence, 54–55
Rio Grande River, xx, 28, 32, 37
Roeder, Otto von, 35 n
Salt, cost of, 46
San Saba River, 38
Santa Fe trade, 36–37
Santa Fe Trail, xxi
Schenk, Fritz, xvii
Schleicher, Gustav, xvii, xviii n. 10
Schubart, Dr. Johann, 44
Separatists, 60
Shakers, colonies of, 60–61
Silesian famine (Germany), 15
Slavery, 12, 23
Society for the Prevention of Pauperism (New York City), 5 n
Society for the Protection of German Immigrants in Texas: founded by German noblemen to promote German emigration to Texas, xv; receives grant of land in Texas, xv; sponsors and signs liberal agreement with Darmstädter group, xvi–xvii; Dr. von Herff appears before Committee of, to report on Bettina

74

Index

experiment and conditions in Texas, xix; Committee receives von Herff manuscript and orders it printed, xix; colonizing operations of, 4; lack of proper financing deplored, 7; criticized by von Herff for 1845–46 immigrant mortality rate in Texas, 14–15; colonizing experience in Texas seen as helpful guideline and assistance for national effort, 28, 35, 62; debts of, 29, 34

Spiess, Hermann, xv–xvii, xxiii n. 10, 61–62

Texas: Society for the Protection of German Immigrants in Texas receives grant of land in, xv; Darmstädter company decides for, xv; described as land of milk and honey, xvi; favored by Ferdinand von Herff, xx: rich land in, xxi; wholesomeness of climate, 12–14; American doctors send patients to, 14; health in, compared to Germany, 15; absence of tuberculosis in, 16; annexation of, 16–17, 37; cotton and wool production possibilities, 23–25; Spanish settlements in, 26–27; banks prohibited under Constitution of 1845, 41; advantages over other states, 67; German settlers as cadre for colonization plan, 67

Texas Rangers, 27–28, 63

Tools and implements: list of, needed by immigrant family, 51; contrasted to European, 52; needed by twenty-family commune, 54, 56

Varrentrapp, Franz, publisher of Frankfurt, Germany: publishes von Herff book, xix

Welschkorn, German word for "corn", 19 n

Wiesbaden, Germany, xvi–xvii

Wisconsin: as site for colonization of Germans, xv; climate compared to Texas, 12–14; further comparisons to Texas as site for colony, 18–21; German settlers in, 67

Wool, production of, 23